THE COMPLETE GUIDE TO CHOOSING CHILD CARE

The National Association of Child Care Resource and
Referral Agencies in cooperation with Child Care, Inc.

THE
COMPLETE
GUIDE
TO
CHOOSING
CHILD CARE

Judith Berezin

RANDOM HOUSE   NEW YORK

Library of Congress Cataloging-in-Publication Data

Berezin, Judith.
   The complete guide to choosing child care/National Association
of Child Care Resource and Referral Agencies in cooperation with
Child Care, Inc.; by Judith Berezin.
      p.   cm.
   Includes index.
   ISBN 0-679-73100-8
   1. Child care—United States.   2. Child care services—United
States.   I. National Association of Child Care Resource and
Referral Agencies.   II. Child Care, Inc.   III. Title.
HQ778.7.U6B47   1991
362.7′12′0973—dc20   90-45487

Manufactured in the United States of America
Book designed by Susan Hood
Children's art coordinated by Collin Leech
First Edition

We thank the following children for contributing art to this book:

The Purple Circle Day Care Center

Sam Dewind ▪ Samuel Rudman ▪ Jesse Krulwich ▪ Benjamin Jacoff ▪
Michael Morales ▪ Rachel Greene ▪ Sasha Mikelewicz ▪ Emily Rosen-King ▪
Ethan Stanislawski ▪ Benjamin Messinger Barnes ▪ Cody Colon-Berezin ▪
Nina Hurwitz ▪ Joya Colon-Berezin

Child Care Dallas—Landauer Child Care Center

Francisco Puebla ▪ Melisa Lopez ▪ Rudy Robledo ▪ Brian Jones ▪ Lauren Higgins
▪ John Phillips ▪ Yassin Ahmed ▪ Gina Avila ▪ Ana Iris Mares ▪
Brannden Poppenberg ▪ Jose Nerio ▪ Kevin Davenport ▪ Ruben Chevez ▪
Jonathan Woodards ▪ Yennys Palomeque ▪ Myrna Garcia ▪ Kenneth Jennings ▪
Jacobie Lacy ▪ Mayra Meza ▪ Jamar Cochran ▪ Gabriela Colunga ▪ Michelle Bason
▪ Mario Martinez ▪ Adrianna Benavides ▪ AshleyAnderson ▪ Edwin Jordan ▪
Demon Smith

Civic League Day Nursery

Jana Larson Keiler ▪ Luke Wrubel ▪ Anne Graner ▪ Jennifer Tran ▪ Jill Thomas

Children's Home Society

Sambath Pech ▪ Jennifer Olson

Other Children

Natahlie Weil ▪ Jonathon Weil ▪ Aaron Neugebauer ▪ Adam Neugebauer ▪
Alex Benepe ▪ Will Maloney

NACCRRA

The National Association of Child Care Resource and Referral Agencies is a national membership organization which promotes the development, maintenance and expansion of quality child care resource and referral services through regional conferences, technical support services and a quarterly newsletter. NACCRRA also provides a national voice for child care resource and referral on issues affecting the quality, accessibility and affordability of child care for all families regardless of income or where they live.

NACCRRA's more than 260 voting members represent child care resource and referral agencies located throughout the country. These agencies offer consultation and information to thousands of parents each month who are seeking assistance in finding the best possible child care for their children. They are available to answer your questions and assist you in your child care search. The names of these agencies can be found in the Appendix of this book.

CHILD CARE, INC.

Child Care, Inc., is the largest child care resource and referral agency serving New York City. Child Care, Inc., provides consultation and information to parents on the full range of child care options, offers training and technical assistance to all types of child care programs, consults with employers and with unions, carries out research, serves as an information resource to policymakers and the media, and organizes advocacy on public child care policies.

Child Care, Inc., like other child care resource and referral agencies, maintains comprehensive information on all legal child care services in New York City including infant/toddler programs, family day care, part- and full-day preschool programs including day care centers, nursery schools and Head Start, school-based pre-kindergarten programs and after-school programs and summer day camps.

Acknowledgments

This book could not have been written without the generous support of members of the board of the National Association of Child Care Resource and Referral Agencies, and the staff of Child Care, Inc. The directory of child care resource and referral agencies was prepared with great care and commitment by Dee Rabehl, NACCRRA's administrative assistant. Arlyce Currie, representing the NACCRRA board, generously gave of her time in giving us feedback on the entire book.

We are grateful to a number of organizations and individuals who shared their time and materials. These included the National Association for the Education of Young Children, the National Association for Family Day Care, Work/Family Directions, Project Home Safe, the Wellesley School Age Child Care Project, and the American Council of Nanny Schools.

A special note of thanks to the children throughout the country, who through their drawings gave us their impressions of child care; and to the parents who shared their personal experiences in making and managing child care arrangements.

Our editor, Charlotte Mayerson, with insight, care, and humor guided us and our dedicated author, Judith Berezin, through the process of translating what we wanted to say into a book that we hope will be a valuable guide for parents as they search for the best possible child care for their children.

Nancy Kolben
Child Care, Inc.
Vice President, NACCRRA

Naomi Sherlock
President, NACCRRA

Contents

THE COMPLETE GUIDE TO CHOOSING CHILD CARE

Introduction

*T*his book is about child care: how to decide what you need, locate it, judge its quality, and make a selection.

We hope to function as your informed companion in a search for child care that can be like a journey through a thorny maze. Parents look for clues to guide them along the way—a 3×5 card on a bulletin board with the name of someone who takes care of children; a telephone number in a want ad; a sign on the lawn of a neighborhood house; a day care center listed in the yellow pages. These may be the leads the parent starts with, only to find that the follow-up phone calls yield a long waiting list or a program that is too expensive or else unacceptable in some other way.

The irony is that at the other end of the maze, there are many dedicated and qualified caregivers and teachers as well as excellent child care programs. Helping you make your way to them is the task of this book.

The major changes in our work force over the past several years have been documented in countless articles and books. The figures are startling: Over 56 percent of all women with children under age six are in the work force, as compared with just over 20 percent in 1970. More than half of all mothers now return to work before their child's first birthday. Women of all ages are entering the work force and remaining in it as permanent workers. Economists project that women will account for two thirds of the net increase in the labor force by the turn of the century and their participation will be critical to meeting the economic needs of the next century.

It was fathers who went out to work and mothers who stayed home with the children in the traditional middle-class American family. The situation has almost completely changed, but unfortunately, child care services have not kept pace with the changes. As a result, parents must make do with situations that do not provide the quality developmental care that every child deserves; with hours that do not coincide with their workday; with decisions that factor cost over quality. They must often settle for patchwork arrangements that are confusing for children and disruptive of the lives of working parents.

As a nation, we profess to cherish family values, but we have allocated far too few resources, either economic or intellectual, to deal with the needs of our families. Obviously, parents need help and it is on their daily struggles that current discussion often focuses. It is, however, our children who are at the center of America's future, and taking care of them properly and lovingly should be among the first priorities of government policy. Because we have not given appropriate economic or professional recognition to those who care for children, many dedicated and qualified people are leaving the field at the very time when we need to expand services.

We are now seeing an increasing awareness of the crucial need for a good child-care-service delivery system. The lack of easily accessible and affordable child care has created a national crisis. Polls indicate that Americans view child care as a primary public policy issue and one that the business community should address as well. Both major national political parties have a child care plank in their platforms, and many child care bills are being debated at the federal and state level.

Child care resource and referral agencies started in the early seventies to bridge the gap between parents seeking child care and those who provide it. These agencies have developed into a core component of the child-care-service delivery system. Their counselors speak with more than 350,000 parents each year about what their child care options are and how best to choose among them. These specially trained people have information about all legally operated child care services in the community. They know what is available, what it costs, and what specific problems parents in their localities may face.

These organizations are also working every day to increase the supply and quality of child care. They recruit and train child care providers and offer technical assistance to family day care providers and local day care centers, as well as providing leadership in efforts to influence public policy.

This book has been prepared under the auspices of the National Association of Child Care Resource and Referral Agencies (NACCRRA), with the cooperation of Child Care, Inc., a leading CCRR agency located in New York City. It was written by an early childhood specialist experienced in working with parents and children. Representatives from around the country who serve on the NACCRRA national board and who themselves are child care experts have reviewed the book's contents and provided anecdotes about child care from people in their communities (and drawings from their children).

NACCRRA represents these more than 260 local resource and referral agencies and provides them with technical support and public policy leadership. It conducts national and regional forums on child care programs and policy.

How to Use This Book

With this book we hope to provide you with a step-by-step guide to locating, evaluating, and selecting child care. The first step is to identify your family's practical needs (Chapter 1). Next, the question is: What are your options? (Chapter 2). Then you will want to figure out what your child needs at this stage of her life (Chapter 3). Next, the book considers, one by one and in close detail, each type of child care and what parents should consider in evaluating it. Suggestions are given for helping your child make a smooth adjustment, and there are also guidelines for maintaining a good relationship with the caregivers and teachers you have chosen. For specific information about child care resource and referral agencies in your area, see pages 203–247. They are listed by state, and the geographic areas they cover are indicated. Call these agencies for help in your own child care search.

If you have a child with special needs, this book may give you some help in your search for child care. It does not, however, deal with the special services that your child might need. You should ask your local child care resource and referral agency for information about such services in your community.

We hope that the information in this book will help make you an informed consumer. You may find that you will have to settle for less than your ideal, but you will have the tools you need to make a good child care choice.

Getting Started

*I*t is difficult to leave your child in someone else's care. The first time you do it may be the hardest, but each time you make a child care decision, you may find yourself wondering: Will it go well? How will my child feel? Have I made the right choice?

The parents we've quoted here express some of their concerns as well as the pleasant surprises they experienced when they went off to work:

I had a lot of anxiety about whether my infant would suffer because nobody could take care of the baby at six weeks or six months as well as I could.

The provider I had really helped me because I don't have any family here, no one to ask when I don't know what to do. My mother is far away, and my mother-in-law, too. The provider was sort of the grandmotherly type. She was good for Eileen, but she also helped me a lot as a parent.

I feel real comfortable with the woman I take my daughter to, and Mariah, she went right for it. Even with my aunt, she cried and cried and didn't want to be left, but with this other person, she just took right to it. Right now I say, "Mariah, I'll be going," and she's fine. But the truth is, I don't really like it because she calls *her* Mom and she calls *her* husband Dad.

I had a lot of misgivings about leaving my son when he was an infant, but I didn't have any choice. My husband and I split up shortly after the baby was born and I had to earn a living. So I just kind of steeled myself and said this is it, this is what you have to do. And he's adjusted well. I can't say I really have major regrets about going back to work. In fact I think maybe it was better, considering everything else that was going on in my life at the time, because my work environment was very supportive—and I think that probably made my time with my son better.

It is natural to feel some ambivalence even if you are eager to return to work. When you have no choice about going, it can be even harder to deal with the necessary separation. You may be leaving a very young infant. Perhaps you've been at home for your child's first few years but now need care for a preschooler. In some instances, your first experience with child care may not come until your child is already in elementary school and you need coverage for the early mornings and late afternoons.

It is easier to go about finding child care if you have support from those around you. If members of your family or your friends question what you are doing, you may feel pressure to justify your decision.

Whatever your child's age, finding the child care situation that will best meet your family's needs can be a challenge. If you go about it carefully and in an organized way, you are more likely to make a good choice. How should you begin?

The first thing to do is figure out your family's practical needs. If you have access to a child care resource and referral agency (see page 203), the counselors there will explain to you what your options are. With their help or on your own, it's best to begin with the nuts-and-bolts issues.

The following questions will help you think about your basic needs:

- When must you begin the arrangement?
- How old will your child be?

- What hours of care do you need, including time to get to work and back? Are the hours fixed or varied? Do you ever have need for overnight child care?
- What days of the week must you cover?
- How much can you afford to pay?
- Are you looking for an arrangement that would be appropriate for one year or the next two to three years?
- Do you need care year-round? Ten months? Eleven months?
- Do you have access to transportation, or would it be better to have someone at home or care within walking distance?
- Would you consider care near your workplace?
- Do you have more than one child? Are their needs and schedules different? Will your older child have to be picked up from school?

Now, go through your list again, looking at your requirements more specifically. Try to figure out which of these factors are absolutes and which might have some flexibility.

For instance, you might have decided that you need care from 7:30 A.M. to 6:30 P.M. in order to get back and forth from work on time. Is there a chance that either you or your spouse can change your work hours slightly if you cannot find care that fits that schedule?

Think about the amount you have decided you can pay. Is it fixed, or could you pay a little more in order to find the care that meets your needs?

If you have decided that you need care for all twelve months of the year, is there a chance you could make a different arrangement in the summer if year-round care is not available?

Once you've decided what the absolute necessities are, you won't waste time pursuing arrangements that clearly couldn't meet your basic needs.

You will learn very soon in your search that good child care services are expensive. Plan to take advantage of the federal child and dependent care tax credit, which is available to all working families whose child care meets certain IRS requirements. You claim the tax credit when you file your income tax returns.

Parents can claim up to $2,400 in child care expenses for one child and $4,800 for two or more children. The credit represents a percentage of these expenses and it declines as your income increases. For a full explanation of the child and dependent care tax credit and regulations governing it, call 1-800-424-FORM and ask for a copy of Form 2441 and Publication 503, Child and Dependent Care Expenses.

You may be able to get other financial help for child care. Some employers have established dependent care assistance plans to help employees pay for child care with pretax dollars. Contact your company's personnel or human resources department to see if such assistance is available. There are usually specific rules governing eligibility, enrollment dates and other qualifying factors.

What Do You Want from a Child Care Arrangement?

You've considered what you *need* in a child care arrangement. Now it's time to think about what you *want*, about the quality of the child care you are seeking. Indulge yourself a little. If you could embellish your list, what might you add?

- Consider particular qualities about a caregiver or teacher—such as age, education, and experience—that are important to you.
- Think about whether you would prefer a small, informal situation with a single caregiver or a bigger, more formal program in a child care center. Would you want your child by himself, with other children his own age, or in a mixed-age setting?
- Think about your own educational philosophies. How might these affect your child care choice?
- If you have more than one child, what kind of care would be best for each one?

Now that you have an idea of what you need and want, your next consideration should be the *type* of care that would be best. The following chapter will describe your options.

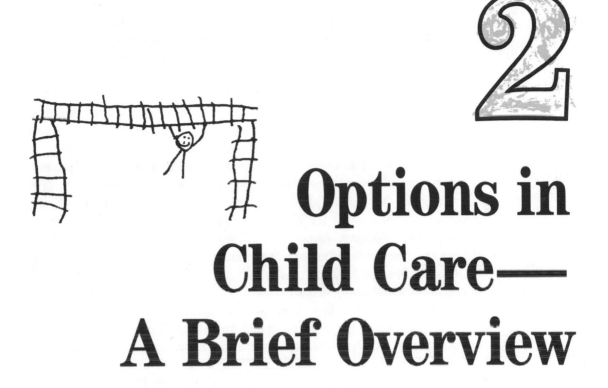

Options in Child Care— A Brief Overview

Now you are ready to look at the types of child care that may be available to you. The option that traditionally comes to mind is family. If your mother, mother-in-law, sister, or brother is available and interested in caring for your child, that may be a good solution for your child care needs.

Leaving your child with someone who knows and loves her can make the separation easier for you both. A family member may share your attitudes about child rearing and give you a feeling of confidence that things will be handled the way you yourself would do it. Care within your family might cost nothing at all, or a lot less than you would have to pay an outside person.

There can be a downside to such an arrangement, however, and it's important to consider these possibilities before you make a decision. If you do have disagreements about your child's care—what she* should eat, when and how to start toilet training, what kind of discipline is appropriate—it may be far more complicated to address these concerns with a family member. You may feel more intimidated about insisting things be done your way and not speak out. Or you may confront the problem and risk causing conflict in a relationship that's very important to you. Your mother or mother-in-law may adore her grandchild and be anxious to provide care. But will she have the energy to keep up with a baby or young child every day for long hours? The question of payment can be an awkward one as well. It may seem strange to pay members of your family for looking after your child; they might even be insulted by the idea. Yet paying for child care, even with a family member, can make the arrangement more formal and reliable and prevent bad feelings on either side. If you decide to leave your child with a relative, it's best to talk frankly about what you both expect and how you will handle problems should they arise.

For most families, however, this isn't even an option. Relatives work or live far away. Most of us have to go outside the family circle to find appropriate child care. There are basically three options: in-home care, family day care, and center care. What you will be able to find depends, to a large degree, on where you live. You might think that one type would be best for you and simply not be able to find it. For that reason, right from the start, it's a good idea to familiarize yourself with all the possibilities.

The following brief descriptions will give you basic facts about each type of care and some of the pros and cons to consider. No particular type of care is inherently better than the others. It will depend on your child's age, what you can afford, and what's available. In any case, the type matters less than the *quality* of the care that's provided.

These summaries will describe your options. Chapter 4 will give you detailed information on in-home care. In Chapter 5 you will find details on finding and using family day care. Chapters 6, 7, and 8 will give you information on center care for infants, toddlers, preschoolers, and school-age children.

* Please note that we have alternated the use of *she* and *he* for children throughout the book and, to a lesser extent, for caregivers.

In-home Care

When you hire someone to work *in your home*, specifically to take care of your children, that is called in-home care. It is an employer-employee relationship where you set the hours, the responsibilities, and the rate of pay. You may want the caregiver to perform duties other than child care, such as housekeeping, laundry, or cooking. You can hire a care-giver to work part-time or full-time or to live in your house. In some cases, one or more families may get together to hire an in-home care-giver for a "shared-care" arrangement in one family's home, or rotated on a weekly or monthly basis from home to home.

In-home caregivers are referred to by a number of different titles: baby-sitters, nannies, au pairs, caregivers, and mother's helpers. You can look for an in-home caregiver on your own or go through agencies that specialize in placing people in these positions.

Possible Advantages of In-home Care:

- If you have an infant or toddler, in-home care will provide continuity in his environment and eliminate the trouble of early-morning and late-evening travel.
- Your child will be able to follow his own schedule for meals, naps, and playtimes.
- If you have two children, one very young and the other in elementary school, an in-home caregiver can care for your older child after school and on days when he is ill or school is closed.
- If someone is working in your house, you will have coverage when your child is sick or there are holidays and school vacations.
- If you have unusual work hours—start very early or get home late— you may be able to find a caregiver who can accommodate.

Possible Disadvantages of In-home Care:

- If the in-home caregiver is late, sick, or leaves without enough notice, you can be stuck.
- Unless you specifically make arrangements with the caregiver to in-volve your child with other children, your child may be isolated.
- There are no particular qualifications or licenses required for in-home caregivers, so you must rely solely on your own judgment.

- The caregiver may not be skilled in engaging your child in a variety of activities.
- If your child is not yet verbal, you may not be sure exactly how he is spending his time with the caregiver.
- In many areas, in-home care is extremely expensive.

Family Day Care

Family day care is the name given to an arrangement in which your child is cared for in the caregiver's home. It can be an informal agreement negotiated between you and a neighbor or friend or an arrangement you find through a CCRR agency or a community organization or by advertising on your own.

The family day care provider may care only for your child and her own or she may run a program for a small group of children. Family day care can be used for part-time or full-time care and in some cases may include overnight care.

In a family day care arrangement, regardless of its formality or informality, the provider is running a business and you are the consumer. Although a great deal may be open to negotiation, it is the provider who will ultimately determine the fees, hours, and program that she will provide.

Possible Advantages of Family Day Care:

- Your child may be more comfortable in a home setting than in a center.
- If there are other children in the family day care home, your child will have playmates.
- If you have unusual work hours, the family day care provider may offer care that can begin early and include breakfast and go on late to include supper.
- If there are regulations governing family day care where you live, you can use a provider who has met licensing requirements.
- If you have an older child in school, the family day care provider may be able to pick her up and provide care for the after-school hours and days when school is closed.

- In some areas, family day care is less expensive than either in-home or center care.
- A family day care provider may be willing to provide care when a child is mildly ill.

Possible Disadvantages of Family Day Care:

- If the provider or her child is sick and she doesn't have backup care, you may be stuck.
- If your child is sick, you may not be able to take her to the family day care home and you are, again, stuck.
- If there are no licensing requirements where you live or few licensed providers, you will be totally on your own to evaluate the safety and quality of the care provided.
- The provider may change the hours or days of care she can offer and these may not meet your needs.
- If the provider is caring for too many children, your child may not get the attention she needs.
- The provider may not have the skills and materials necessary to offer your child a variety of age-appropriate activities.
- If the provider doesn't have her own yard and is caring for a group of children, it may be difficult for her to take them out to a park or playground.

Center Care

Center care is group care that takes place outside a home setting. A child care center may exist on its own or be run by a larger organization, such as a church, synagogue, community center, or business. Early childhood centers, serving three-, four- and five-year-old children, are the most prevalent. There are, however, an increasing number of programs for infants and toddlers. There are also centers that care for school-age children during the late-afternoon hours.

In the past, the most common center programs were nursery schools. They offered either a morning or afternoon program for three- and four-year-olds and were designed to provide a social and educational experience, not child care for working parents. This is no longer generally the case. Many nursery schools, like day care centers, now offer full-day programs geared to working parents. All *good* center programs, regardless of what they are called, are designed to provide a balanced social and educational experience for young children.

Possible Advantages of Center Care:

- Center care is usually regulated and inspected to set minimum standards for health, safety, and group size.
- Centers often have on their staffs directors and teachers who have studied child development.
- Your child will be with other children at a center.
- The center will provide care even if your child's teacher is absent.
- Centers may offer greater variety in the materials and activities they have available.
- Most centers include outdoor play as part of their daily schedule.
- It is unlikely that a center will close without a fair amount of advance notice to parents.

Possible Disadvantages of Center Care:

- Centers have specific hours that may not match your own.
- Your child will probably have to conform to a schedule for meals, snacks, and naps that may be difficult for him.
- If your child is sick, you cannot take him to the center and you will have to find alternative care.
- If the group is large and there are not enough teachers, your child may not get the individual attention he needs.
- Most centers close for certain holidays and vacations—some for the entire summer—so you will have to make other arrangements.
- In some areas center care, particularly for infants and toddlers, is very expensive.

You may already have a preference for one type of care and, to proceed to the next step, you may want to go right to the chapter of this book that covers it. We suggest, however, that you read about all the options that might be appropriate for your child before you make a specific decision about what to pursue.

Bear in mind also that children of different ages have different needs. This is what we will consider in the next chapter.

3

Your Child's Developmental Needs

*A*s you consider possible child care options, pay particular attention to the stage of development your child is in. In this chapter we will consider the needs of infants and toddlers in some detail, because care for children under three is often the most difficult to find and the least regulated. The needs of older children are mentioned later in the chapter, with references to parts of the book where they are discussed in depth.

The first guidelines we offer are designed to focus your attention on what your very young child needs from *any* person who takes care of him whether in your home, the provider's home, or a center. What are some of the most important experiences for a baby or toddler? How can caregivers* best support healthy development in these early years? In

* To simplify matters we have, in most cases, used only the term *caregiver*. However, some family day care providers and staff at infant/toddler centers are fully qualified teachers.

the following sections we will discuss in detail the specific qualities and skills a caregiver should have to respond appropriately to your developing child.

What Do Babies Need?

The simple and most direct answer is: a lot of attention. Babies cannot wait for food, comfort, changing, or holding. They do not have the resources to ease tension in their bodies when they are in discomfort. They are dependent on others to make them feel good again and need a quick and loving response when in distress.

Consistency

Your baby should have consistency in the style of care she receives and from whom she receives it. This means she needs someone specially interested in her, who "belongs" to her and will be there when she calls. If she gets this kind of reliable response to her needs, she will develop a sense of trust in her environment and see the world as a predictable and friendly place.

Physical Care

The caregiver should be comfortable with the physical aspects of baby care and should handle your baby's body gently and respectfully. Feeding, diapering, and dressing should be opportunities for social interaction, learning, and fun. It is also essential for your baby's good health that the people who care for her follow certain procedures: washing hands before feeding and after diapering the baby; making sure bottles, nipples, and toys are kept clean; serving food and formula at the right temperature; refrigerating unused formula and baby food and discarding them when they are no longer fresh; changing diapers promptly when the baby is wet or soiled; cleaning the baby thoroughly and applying cream when necessary to prevent diaper rash.

Emotional Support

Your baby needs a caregiver who will pay attention to her moods and learn her signals, who will balance the day between stimulating activities and quiet times. When your baby is tired or cranky, she will need the reassuring physical presence of an adult who can hold and soothe her.

When awake and responsive, your baby should be played with and talked to. The caregiver should make frequent eye contact, "mirror" her expressions, talk directly to her, offer her interesting toys to explore.

Your baby needs an enthusiastic audience for her increasing accomplishments. When she begins to make sounds, her caregiver should respond, echoing them back, encouraging her to "talk" more. At other times, when she is feeling content, your baby should have opportunities to play by herself: for example, listening, or watching a mobile turn as she lies in a crib, or sucking and handling toys while sitting in an infant seat.

Mobility

If your baby is still too little to move around on his own, the caregiver should make sure he spends time in different positions—some time on a lap, over the shoulder, in an infant seat, and down on the floor. There should be interesting things to see—simple pictures with clear objects and different colors; a variety of textures for him to touch; toys that shake or rattle or ring in response to his actions. When he begins to crawl, he needs someone to make sure the environment is safe and inviting.

Your baby needs someone who will play with him physically so he can strengthen his developing muscles: helping him clap hands; rotating his legs, bicycle style; pulling him to standing position when he is ready; holding toys within his reach so he can grab them.

Time outdoors is an important part of a baby's day—a chance to look at the world from a baby carrier or a stroller, to crawl on the grass or play in a sandbox. His caregiver should narrate his outdoor adventures, telling him about the trees, people, dogs, and cars that pass them by.

Caring for babies is very hard work. It is also extremely rewarding. It can be done well only by caregivers who are gentle and responsive and genuinely enjoy the company of infants.

What Do Toddlers Need?

The Atmosphere

An environment that will encourage their exploration of the world while providing a safe home base is important for toddlers. They are filled with the excitement of being upright and mobile. They think the world was designed for their pleasure and have little understanding of what anyone else may want. Although they feel very powerful, their new abilities can also frighten them at times. Children of this age want to come and go at their own pace, moving away from the caregiver when it suits them, yet able to return for comfort and "refueling."

Mobility

Your toddler needs space to move about in and to practice his new walking skills. He will enjoy pillows or chairs to climb on, corners to hide in, passages to crawl through. Spending time outside is important: exercising his large muscles, walking, running, sliding, swinging, climbing up and down steps. Toddlers especially love toys that can accompany them on their travels—small carts or carriages to push, toys on strings that can be pulled.

Your toddler needs someone who can set limits calmly and consistently for his safety, showing as well as telling him the safe way to use a toy or approach another child. The caregiver should be alert to steer the toddler away from danger, redirecting his attention to safe and constructive activities.

A child this age will do best when his day is balanced between active and quiet times. Toddlers often tend to go until they drop; stories, music, or quiet games will help them wind down so they can nap or rest.

Language Development

A caregiver who talks directly to him and pays close attention to what he is saying will help your toddler learn to communicate, to make himself understood and expand his use of language. Someone who names objects for the child, reads stories to him, plays with words, and sings songs is an important partner at this stage of development.

Emotional Support

Toddlers need a lot of repetition, as you will surely notice when you are with your child. They want to hear the same story "again," climb the same flight of steps "again," sing the same song "again." A caregiver should understand that this is how a toddler gains mastery over new challenges and should have the patience to do whatever it is "one more time."

Your toddler should be encouraged to do things by herself when she tries to. She may want to get her own cup or put on her own shoe. When she fails in her attempts at independence, which of course she frequently will, she is likely to be very frustrated. A good caregiver will assist and reassure her, breaking the task down into things she can do or offering her a different task she is sure to succeed at. At other times, your toddler will want help; her caregiver should convey that this too is all right.

Children of this age frequently say no and refuse to do what they are told. The caregiver needs to understand that such behavior is not spiteful but a natural and important stage of development. The toddler is experimenting with who she is and trying to assert her separate identity.

Simple and consistent routines are important for toddlers. Your child wants to know how her day will begin, when she will have something to eat, when she will go outside. She should be told what will happen next and given ample time to complete what she is doing.

Mastering New Skills

There should be opportunities to experiment with a variety of materials and toys that feed your child's curiosity and help her master new skills. She can try drawing with large crayons, in her own way, with no pressure to "make something," stacking large cardboard blocks and, if she likes, knocking them down. She should have time to play with water and sand, squashing, pouring, emptying, and filling containers.

Your toddler needs the opportunity to be around other children at times, to explore them under the watchful eye of the caregiver. She will need help in learning how to interact physically and verbally with other children. Her caregiver should model this behavior, guiding her on how to approach her peers and giving her words that will help her make contact.

Physical Care

Because toddlers are very active, with little or no sense of danger, a caregiver must keep constant watch—making sure harmful objects and substances are kept out of reach, that, among other hazards, doorways and staircases are protected and there is no access to a road or parking lot. Children of this age often want to eat in bits and snatches while on the move. Bottles and food get dropped and picked up again. It's important for the caregiver to be prepared—to have extra bottles and snacks to replace what gets dirty.

Toddlers are very curious about their own bodies, what goes in and what comes out. The caregiver should respect your toddler's body and his curiosity about how it is made. It is important that the person who cares for him understand that this curiosity is natural and an important prerequisite to toilet training. She should react to his interest calmly and cheerfully, letting him see what is in his diapers if he wishes. Many children at this stage no longer want to lie down for diaper changes. It can be a challenge to "catch" a busy toddler, but it's important to make sure diapers are changed frequently enough to avoid rashes.

A good caregiver understands that toilet training and weaning from bottles are major milestones for a young child. The child will indicate when or whether he is ready for these steps. If the caregiver thinks he is, she should discuss it with you before proceeding with any plan.

The care of toddlers is physically and emotionally demanding. It is also exciting and rewarding. It can only be done well by caregivers who are patient, flexible, and energetic.

There are still relatively few infant/toddler centers. Most parents are likely to use either in-home or family day care during these early years, though this may change in the future. If you are considering center care, however, you will find additional information on how to evaluate the program and caregivers in Chapter 6, "Infant/Toddler Centers."

What Do Preschool Children Need?

Children between the ages of three and five have some of the same needs as infants and toddlers. Good physical care and a safe and interesting environment are essential. They, too, need consistent and supportive responses from the adults who care for them.

By this point, however, children are usually ready and eager for the companionship of their peers. They will need help and support in the delicate art of making friends and keeping them—learning how to share and take turns, settling disputes with words instead of hitting or grabbing.

Children of this age are also ready for more structured materials and experiences. They need opportunities to work with puzzles, blocks, scissors, crayons, paint, and glue—materials that will help them develop skills they will need later for reading, writing, and math.

In Chapter 7, "Early Childhood Centers," you will find a detailed discussion of the developmental needs of this age group and the kinds of activities that are appropriate whether the children are cared for in centers or in family day care homes.

What Do School-age Children Need?

Children in elementary school need care during after-school hours and on days when schools are closed and parents are at work. After-school care should not be a continuation of the regular school day or merely a way station for custodial care. A well-designed program will take into account differing needs of the individual children involved and offer experiences that may not be included in the regular school day.

Children of this age need to relax a bit, have a snack, kick off their shoes (figuratively, if not literally), just the way they would if they came directly home. Since most school programs keep children fairly confined during the day, some of them will want to stretch their muscles, run, play, be noisy. Others may prefer to unwind with quiet board games or cards.

This is a stage of development when peer relationships take on great significance. Most children of this age are likely to prefer a situation where they are neither isolated nor with children much younger or older.

We will talk more specifically about the developmental needs of this age group and appropriate program design in Chapter 8, "Child Care for School-age Children."

In the following chapters, we will discuss each type of child care in detail. We will look specifically at the kinds of environments and the qualities of caregivers that you should look for in in-home care, family day care, or center-based care. As you think about specific types of care, bear in mind that the developmental needs we have described are general; your child's individual temperament will also be an important factor to consider in your child care choice.

In-home Care

When you hire someone to work in your home to take care of your child, that's in-home care. You will set the hours, responsibilities, and compensation for the job. You can hire someone to work part-time or full-time or to live in your home. The job may sometimes include additional responsibilities, such as housekeeping, laundry, and cooking.

If you live in an area where many people want this kind of work, finding in-home care may not be hard. But even if locating someone to work is a problem where you live, it's important to give yourself time to make a careful choice. You and your child will be establishing an intimate relationship with a new person. You will be taking someone into your home to take care of your child when you and your family are not around.

This Midwest mother expressed what many parents seem to feel:

The first thing that was really tough was reconciling leaving my six-month-old child with somebody else. That was really hard. I mean, I missed her. I had to figure out a way to trust that the caregiver and I could have a relationship and that I would be part of the experience my child was having. After all, she was the substitute mother for my child.

Who Are the Caregivers?

There are many capable women and some men who work as in-home caregivers. They are known as baby-sitters, nannies, caregivers, au pairs, mother's helpers, and housekeepers. Often these titles reflect differences in the way caregivers see themselves and the background that has led them to this work. Some people have chosen a career in child care. They may have studied child development in a nanny-training program or taken education courses in college. These caregivers are less likely to consider a job that involves housework, other than specific tasks related to the care of the child—preparing her meals or cleaning her room after play.

Many people looking for in-home care jobs are recent immigrants. Some have had experience rearing their own children or taking care of other people's children in their native country. Others, with no experience in child care, take in-home care jobs because that is the only kind of work they can find.

What Should the Job Be?

Think carefully about whether you need a housekeeper who will do some child care, or a caregiver, whose main focus of attention will be your child. It is tempting to try to find someone who will be able to "do it all." Realistically, as you know if you have spent time at home with a young child, it is difficult to manage a lot of household chores simultaneously with providing good child care. Consider the age of your child and how much time and attention he or she will need. An infant or toddler who is being taken care of by someone also responsible for vacuuming, laundry, and cooking may spend a lot of time in a crib or playpen or in front of the TV. On the other hand, if your child attends a child care program for part of the day, it may work out well to hire someone full-time who does the housecleaning while the child is away. This would also give you child care coverage on days when the program is closed or your child is sick.

What Kind of Caregiver Are You Looking For?

Do you want someone to live in? If your hours are irregular, you have more than one child, or you must travel frequently, a live-in caregiver could be the best solution for your child care needs.

There are definite advantages to this type of arrangement:

- Many families find that live-in care gives them the most flexibility and continuity, particularly if very young children are involved.
- You do not have to worry about your caregiver showing up in the morning or being on time.
- You probably won't have to make additional child care arrangements to go out for an evening or to travel.
- Since you will probably spend time with the caregiver and your child, you may have fewer anxieties about how things are handled when you aren't at home.
- You will be able to share information about your child in an ongoing, informal way.

Live-in care provides a good child care solution for many working families. There are, though, possible disadvantages to bringing another person into your household. If you are considering live-in care, think carefully about the following practical questions:

- Do you have the space in your home or apartment to accommodate an additional person? Would she have her own room or sleep in your child's room? Do you have an extra bathroom or would she share yours?
- Would you have to make alterations in your house or apartment in order to accommodate another person? What would they cost?
- Live-in caregivers generally expect to earn as much as those who live out. Salaries vary, depending upon the caregiver's experience, training, and where you live. In large cities and the areas surrounding them, current rates range from $200 a week for a relatively inexperi-

enced person to $400 a week for a highly qualified caregiver. In rural areas or places with large numbers of recent immigrants, you might pay considerably less, perhaps between $100 and $200 a week.

This mother got right to the heart of the matter:

I live in New York, and paying for child care is like a second rent. And most of the time you get what you pay for. A lot of people are providing wonderful care for kids, but when I talk to people and they say, "Oh, my care is cheap," I wonder how they can find someone who will do a wonderful job without a decent salary.

It's important to consider the personal dynamics of bringing an additional person into your household. How much a part of the family would you want her to be? For instance, would you expect her to have meals with you? Sometimes? All the time? If you are home in the evenings and want time alone with your children, would you expect her to stay in her room or to go out?

This mother raises a subtle but important point:

I remember I was so excited we were having this party for my son's first birthday. I had someone taking care of him at home at the time, and he was much more interested in spending time with this person than with me. And I still remember this feeling of distress—I was very jealous of this kind of attachment. I think it's something parents feel a lot and they don't always know what to do with those feelings.

If the caregiver is a young person, might you feel some parental responsibilities? Will you be comfortable not knowing what she does on her time off, feel some concern about where she is, whom she is with, or when she gets home?

If she is an older, more mature woman who has reared her own children, might you feel that she is judging your parental skills? Will you find it hard to give her instructions? To have things done your way?

Even if the caregiver has her own room, she will no doubt hear your family talking, playing, and fighting. How would you feel about this?

Many of these issues are very personal, depending a great deal on the kind of life-style you have and how important your privacy is to you. Talk these issues over thoroughly in the family so that if you do decide to have someone live in, you will be clear about the kinds of guidelines that would work.

What Will the Caregiver's Responsibilities Be?

Whether you are looking for live-in help or someone who will work for you only during the day, it's important to think very specifically about the actual responsibilities you will require from a caregiver.

Some questions to consider are:

- Do you expect the caregiver to do other things in addition to child care? Shopping, cooking, cleaning, laundry? Just for your child or for the entire family?
- Does she need to be able to drive?
- Will she have to bring or pick up your child from any sort of child care program, school, or other activities, like music lessons, dance classes, dentist's or doctor's appointments?
- If your family has pets, will the caregiver have responsibilities for their care?

As you outline the tasks that need to be performed, think about what is important to you in terms of the caregiver's qualifications:

- Do you want the person to have had some formal training in child care and child development? First aid?
- What level of education matters to you? Do you want someone who can read stories to your toddler? Help an older child with homework?
- Would you prefer a caregiver who has had experience with children the age of your child?
- Would you feel more comfortable if she has children of her own?
- Is it important that she be fluent in your language?

In some parts of the country the majority of women seeking in-home positions are immigrants, with varying degrees of proficiency in English. Many families find it a positive experience to have their child exposed to a second language, but you need to think about it carefully. Is it important that the person you hire know *some* English? Be interested in learning more? Are you willing to learn another language? Will you find it possible to explain what you want to explain? Will your child be able to make his needs understood? Bear in mind that you will sometimes need to communicate detailed information to your caregiver, particularly if very young children are involved.

Think also about the personal qualities that matter to you:

- Do you have particular feelings about the age or sex of the caregiver? Are you looking for an energetic young person who can play actively with your toddler or a more mature person, with years of experience? If your children do not have grandparents available, might being with an older woman be a positive experience for them? If you are a woman alone with your children, would a male caregiver provide a nurturing role model?
- Do you have strong feelings about habits related to health care? Would you mind if she smokes? Is her personal grooming important to you? Are there particular types of food your family uses or avoids? Would you want her to follow your dietary plan?
- Think about your attitudes on child rearing: In what areas must hers be compatible? Consider the kinds of behavior you encourage and discourage in your children and what kinds of influences would work in harmony with your ideas. What methods of discipline are acceptable to you? Think about your family's style of interaction. Would you be more comfortable with someone who is talkative and outgoing or someone who is more reserved and quiet?
- Do you have strong feelings about your house being kept in a certain way? Will it bother you if the caregiver is not as neat as you are or if she is more concerned with neatness and order than you are?
- Does your family have certain attitudes about religion? What if the caregiver has different views? Would you be comfortable if her religious beliefs affected her style of child care or things that she said to your child?

Finding an In-home Caregiver

If you have access to a child care resource and referral agency (see page 203), the counselors there can assist you in your search. They may be able to give you names of potential caregivers and/or guide you to appropriate employment agencies and nanny schools. Many CCRRs maintain profiles on agencies, outlining the services they provide. They also collect feedback from parents on their experiences, so they may be able to give you some guidance about agencies, newspapers to advertise in, and the cost of in-home care in your community.

Finding the right caregiver will take time and organization whether you search through agencies, on your own, or both. Talk to several candidates before you decide, and try to "get the word out" that you're looking.

Going Through Employment Agencies

Agencies that place in-home caregivers are usually found in cities or their nearby suburbs. They vary a great deal in size and style, from small companies run by one or two people to businesses with large staffs, handling a broad range of placements. Many agencies recruit caregivers from around the country, lately from the Midwest. Some of these applicants are genuinely interested in pursuing careers in child care; for others, the job may simply be a way to leave home and see another part of the country.

Agency personnel often have great respect for caregivers and try to ensure that they are treated fairly. They select applicants carefully, and screen employers pretty thoroughly as well, trying to make a good match between families and caregivers. There are, however, agencies that accept virtually all applicants and aim to make placements as quickly and simply as possible. They may talk as if they have an "us and them" mentality, seeing the caregivers as quasi servants and referring to them as if they are children you need to handle. It's a good idea to ask other parents about various agencies to find out their reputations rather than just calling those listed in the phone book.

When you do contact an agency, be as explicit as possible about your needs. Find out how the agency recruits applicants and what kind of screening is done. How many references are required? How thoroughly are they checked? Does the agency give any type of training or orientation or does it simply list the names of any interested applicants? Ask how soon you should expect to hear from applicants and how the agency expects you to proceed. Are you to call the agency after you meet each applicant? If you like someone, do you hire her directly or does the agency handle the employment agreement?

Agencies will charge you a fee for their services. They may ask for a percentage of the first month's wages or for two- to four-weeks' salary. Find out exactly how the policy works. Will your money be refunded if the arrangement doesn't work out? Will the agency find someone else for you without further charge if the caregiver leaves within a certain period of time? Does the agency expect a specific salary for its caregivers? Get the full picture of how each agency you contact works.

Frequently, agencies will advertise that they handle both live-out and live-in help, but they may not actually have any caregivers looking for live-in jobs when you call. Currently, the demand for live-in help is far greater than the supply. If you have decided that you need a live-in caregiver, there are a few other options open to you.

Nanny Schools

Not every agency with the word *nanny* in its title offers training to its applicants. There are, however, schools specifically set up to recruit, train, and place women as nannies. Many of these women are looking for live-in jobs. If you want to hire someone from such a program, the American Council of Nanny Schools (see page 201) maintains a listing of programs that have met their criteria for curriculum and training. These are their current guidelines:

The program must have a minimum of two hundred contact hours and one hundred field work hours. These include instructional lectures, field trips, and discussions under supervision of faculty. Field experiences are defined as supervised, unpaid work experiences with children.

The core curriculum should include:

Child growth and development
Family dynamics/interpersonal skills
Health and safety
Nutrition
The nanny as a professional
Practicum

Au Pair Programs

Another option for finding a live-in caregiver is to participate in a government-authorized au pair program. These programs have been designed as a cultural exchange for young Europeans interested in coming to America to study. In exchange for this opportunity, the au pair provides up to forty-five hours a week of child care. Careful screening is done on both ends. Au pairs must be eighteen to twenty-five years old, in good health, have completed secondary school, and have some prior experience working with young children. You must prove through applications and interviews that you have a genuine interest in hosting a young foreigner. You will be expected to provide opportunities for her or him to take certain courses and learn about America. The arrangement has a one-year limit, which cannot be extended. A list of approved au pair programs can be found on page 202.

Recent immigration laws have been designed to discourage parents from making this kind of arrangement except through such formal programs. Trying to bring over a young foreigner on your own is now virtually impossible, though it was quite common a few years ago. (See page 43 for U.S. Department of Justice guidance.)

Looking on Your Own

Even if you decide to go through an agency, it is still worthwhile to explore other sources in your search. One of your friends or co-workers may have a terrific caregiver they no longer need. Or their caregiver may have a friend or relative looking for work. Spread the word early in your search. Many families have found wonderful caregivers through this type of networking.

Other avenues to pursue:

- Talk with other parents and caregivers in local parks and playgrounds, community centers, schools—wherever you run into them.
- Ask for recommendations from your pediatrician and obstetrician.
- Post notices on local community bulletin boards, in churches, synagogues, day care centers, and YMCAs.*
- Advertise in local papers. Ask which papers are good for finding this kind of person. In your ad, be explicit about the hours you need and the qualifications you are seeking.

---

* To simplify matters we have referred to YMCAs throughout this book. This is meant to include YWCAs, YMHAs, and YWHAs as well.

■ Advertise in large papers . . . but be prepared for a huge response. Regardless of what your ad actually says, you will probably get calls from people who do not meet your qualifications at all. Specify the times that you will accept calls. Use an answering machine if you can, so you will have some selectivity about whom you call back and when.

Screen Applicants by Telephone

Telephone screening will help you eliminate many unsuitable applicants. Because you may speak with a great many individuals, it is helpful to draw up a little form that will allow you to note basic information quickly and to keep different applicants straight in your mind. Make several copies of the form and keep a stack handy by the phone.

CAREGIVER SCREENING FORM

Referred by: _____ Date: _____

Name: _____ Phone: _____

Interested in job as described: Yes _____ No _____

Previous experience: _____

_____

_____

References:

Name _____ Phone _____

Name _____ Phone _____

Interview: time _____ date _____

General impressions:

At the beginning of the call, find out if the applicant is interested and available for the specific hours you need and whether she will work within the salary range you have in mind. If not, don't proceed any further.

If the hours and salary seem satisfactory, ask about her background and what she enjoys about working with children. Ask about her last job and why she left it. Tell her that you need at least two references, and notice how she responds. She should be prepared for this question and have names, addresses, and phone numbers readily available.

If you feel that she is a strong candidate, you may want to set up an interview right away. Remember, this person is job hunting, so your timing may be an important factor. If you have mixed feelings, tell her that you are talking with a number of applicants and will get back to her if you want to set up an interview. It is a good idea to check references *before* meeting the caregiver. This will help give you some basis for discussion in the interview and will mean you don't waste time meeting people with poor references.

Sometimes the people who sound best on the phone may disappoint you, as was the case for this mother:

The ad I placed in a local paper got a huge response. The phone wouldn't stop ringing. But it was very discouraging. People didn't have the right qualifications, references, or attitude. Then I got a call from a young woman who sounded perfect. We must have talked for an hour. I set up an interview and then went off into fantasy land. We would love her; she would love my kids. I could see her in the family album. The day she was coming, I got up early, cleaned my whole house, and baked muffins. Then I waited . . . and waited . . . and waited. . . . She never came. Never even called.

It is not uncommon for applicants to fail to show up for interviews. Even if you have wonderful conversations with a couple of prospective caregivers, it's a good idea to plan to meet at least four or five possible candidates.

Checking References

No matter who referred you to this caregiver—even if an agency has checked her references—it is essential that you contact the references directly. Ask for at least two. When you call, tell the person that you understand it might make her uncomfortable if there is anything negative to be said, but it is very important to you to make a good decision and you will really appreciate her honesty. Listen to the way she responds as well as to what she actually says. Is her tone enthusiastic? Hesitant? Does she seem uncomfortable about discussing her experiences? Ask very specific questions!

Find out:

- When and for how long did the caregiver work in her last position?
- What were the ages of the children in her care?
- How did the children feel about her?
- What were her specific duties? Did she have any problems meeting those responsibilities?
- Was she punctual and reliable?
- How was her health?
- What was the relationship like? Were there ever disagreements? How were they resolved?
- Why did she leave?

The importance of checking references cannot be stated strongly enough. What you learn may be pivotal in your decision. You may turn up a piece of information that can save you from making a terrible mistake or cause you to reconsider a hasty first impression after hearing what other parents have to say:

When I first met the woman who's taking care of my kid, I wasn't at all sure about her. I mean, she seemed competent but she didn't give off any warmth. But then I started calling her references and they were unbelievable. I mean, I kept saying, "Are you sure, are you sure? Are you friends with this woman?" Because it was like, you know, she was better to the kids than I was . . . People were saying those kinds of things. And she *was* wonderful. I mean, I could not have found a better person to take care of my child.

Interviews

Interviews can be an awkward experience for both people involved, though they get easier the more of them you do. Some parents find it helpful to have a friend with them or for both parents to be present when meeting prospective caregivers.

Invite the applicant to come at a time when your children are present. There are many questions to ask her and a good deal of information you will want to know, but you will learn a great deal by watching how she handles this initial interaction with you and your children. Do not push your child to relate to the caregiver or vice versa. Simply make an introduction and watch what unfolds.

Someone who is skilled with young children will find the moment and means to engage them. Observe how the caregiver approaches your child. Does she take her cues from your child's behavior? Does she respond appropriately to your child's actions and reactions?

Talk with her about her previous experiences and ask her why she enjoys working with children. Tell her a little about your child and pay attention to what kinds of questions she asks. A good interview should be a two-way street. Does she ask about the child's schedule, temperament, likes, and dislikes?

Think about your child's age and the kind of behavior this caregiver is likely to encounter. Try to find out how close her attitudes are to yours. This mother explains how important that can be:

We have had a number of different types of people taking care of my child in our home, and one experience was bad. During the potty-training process, when he would go in his pants, she would tell him he was a bad boy. It became such a strong statement to him that all the horror stories about toilet training came true and we had a big issue with it.

Encourage the applicant to talk about her experiences with children. Try to find out how much she understands about the developmental needs of children the age of yours. Tell her about your child's behavior, and ask how she would handle the situations you describe. If you find it difficult to get her talking, it may be helpful to have some very specific questions to get the ball rolling.

If you have an infant, you might ask:
- Does she think the baby should be picked up whenever he cries?
- Does she think it's important for a baby to go outside every day?
- What does she think infants need most from a caregiver?
- What kinds of activities would she do with your baby?
- Does she think it's important to talk to a young infant?

If you have a toddler, you might ask:

- When and how should toilet training be introduced?
- How would she handle a temper tantrum?
- What activities would she try on a rainy day?
- Where and how often would she take the child out?
- What toys does she think are good for toddlers?

If you have a preschool child, you might ask:

- What indoor and outdoor activities she would plan?
- What kind of discipline does she think is appropriate if a child misbehaves?
- What are her favorite children's books?
- What television shows, if any, does she think are appropriate?
- Does she believe children this age need to spend time with peers? Would she be willing to supervise play dates or take your child to an activity group?

If you have a school-age child, you might ask:

- Would she take your child outside to play after school?
- Would she be able and willing to help with homework?
- How would she feel about having your child's friends come over after school?
- On days when school is closed, what kind of activities would she plan?

Even if the interview goes well, it's best not to make a job offer on the spot. If you have very positive feelings, you should certainly indicate that, but give yourself a little time to think it over. Tell the applicant you will get back to her within a day or two. If your spouse was not present at the first interview, you may want to arrange a second one. If your child is old enough, you should certainly explore with him how he felt about the person.

Making Your Decision

You may have to talk with several people before you find the right person. If you are uneasy about someone *for any reason*, do not hire her, even if her answers are "good" and her references check out. Trust your instincts! Remember, this person will be in your home, with your child. You will be extremely dependent upon her, so it is essential that you like her and feel that she is trustworthy. Base your decision on what you have seen in her interactions with your child, what her references said, and how you felt talking with her. It is unlikely that you will find a "perfect" person, one who meets all of your criteria. The most important thing is that you feel that she would take good care of your child.

When you have found a caregiver you want to hire, the two of you will need to discuss conditions of employment. The following section will give you guidelines on your obligations and expectations as an employer.

Becoming an Employer

It is natural to want an easygoing, comfortable relationship with someone who spends a lot of time with your child. You may worry that if you act too much like a boss, this will be reflected in the caregiver's attitude toward your child. You are less likely to run into awkward situations that can disrupt a pleasant relationship if clear, fair agreements are made at the outset.

No matter how informal and personal your relationship may become, if you are paying someone to care for your child on a regular basis, in your home, you have created an employer/employee relationship.

As an employer you have legal obligations to fulfill. For the most up-to-date information on all reporting requirements, contact your accountant or tax consultant or call the IRS at 1-800-424-FORM. Ask them to send you all the forms that you will need for household employees. The IRS Publication 503, Child and Dependent Care Expenses, includes all of the applicable forms and an explanation of how to complete them. Many of the key reporting and insurance requirements are listed below.

Social Security

If you pay an individual more than $50 in a calendar quarter, those wages are subject to Social Security taxes under the Federal Insurance Contribution Act (FICA). Both you and your employee are obligated to pay a designated portion of the tax, though in practice many employers cover the entire cost themselves. If you do pay both parts, you must list the employee share as additional taxable income on your employee's year-end W-2 form. Taxes are due quarterly and must be submitted with IRS Form 942, on which you report your caregiver's wages.

Income Tax

You do not have to withhold federal income tax from your caregiver's paycheck. If you choose to, you should report the amounts withheld on the IRS Form 942 for Social Security. Whether or not income tax is withheld, you must give the caregiver a W-2 form for the previous year's earnings by January 31. Form W-3 must be used to send a copy of your caregiver's W-2 to the IRS.

You will need to obtain an employer identification number to report employment taxes and give tax statements to your employee. You can obtain a number by filing form SS-4 with the IRS.

You may also be responsible for withholding city and state taxes. Check with your accountant or local officials for the requirements in your area.

Unemployment Compensation

If you pay a caregiver $1,000 or more in a calendar quarter, you are required to pay Federal Unemployment Tax (FUTA). Payments are reported annually to the IRS using form 940. States vary on the specific requirements and rates for unemployment taxes. For this information, it is best to contact the state unemployment office in your area. Look in the local phone book for this office. In most cases, if you must pay the state, you can take a credit against your federal unemployment tax.

Workers' Compensation

Laws governing workers' compensation vary from state to state. First check with your own insurance broker to find out if you are covered for workers' compensation through your homeowners insurance policy. In some states you are required to have a separate policy. Your insurance agent should be able to give you this information and tell you whom to contact if you need more information.

Car Insurance

Your caregiver may have to be added to your insurance policy and her driving record may have to be checked. Ask your insurance agent about your state's requirements.

Paying "Off the Books"

It has been very common for a long time to pay caregivers in cash, "off the books." This gave the caregiver more income and freed parents from dealing with paperwork required in filing taxes. This has never been a legal arrangement and the Internal Revenue Service is now pursuing this form of tax evasion.

Should your caregiver decide at some future time to file for Social Security and if she can prove prior earnings, you could be liable for years' worth of unpaid taxes, interest, and penalties. In addition, you cannot claim the child care tax credit when filing your own income tax or take advantage of a tax exclusion for dependent care (DCAP), if your employer offers this option, unless you meet all the legal requirements outlined in the previous pages.

Employment Requirements

Sometimes caregivers who are recent immigrants do not have legal status to work in this country. If you've found a good person, it may be tempting to hire her anyhow. It's important, however, to consider the possible consequences.

In 1986 Congress passed sweeping new legislation regarding the employment of individuals who are not citizens. As an employer you are required to verify that any individual you hire is eligible to work here legally or is an American citizen. It is not enough to ask your caregiver if she is a citizen or has a green card. You are required to complete the U.S. Immigration and Naturalization Services Form I-9 for any individual whom you hire. Both you and the caregiver must sign this form. In addition you must see actual proof of eligibility for employment. This includes a Social Security card, U.S. passport, alien registration card, and some form of picture identification such as a driver's license or student ID card. For copies of the form or for more information, contact the U.S. Department of Justice Immigration and Naturalization Service. You may face substantial fines if you do not comply with the requirements of this law.

Salary

A caregiver who works in your home is entitled to earn at least the current federal minimum wage. In practice, most caregivers earn more. A caregiver's rate generally depends on several factors: her previous experience and expertise, the responsibilities you have given her, whether she is affiliated with an agency, and what the "going rate" is in your area. As we have mentioned, you are likely to pay at least $200 a week and perhaps as much as $400 for in-home care in most cities, though you may pay less in rural areas or small towns.

Overtime

Any hours that go beyond your usual arrangement should be considered overtime. In general, overtime should be paid at the rate of time-and-a-half. Though it can be more complicated to arrange, another option to consider is compensatory time—giving the caregiver time off with pay in exchange for the extra hours worked. Make sure that the issue of overtime has been settled before the need arises, so you are both clear on how it is to be handled.

Raises

A good in-home caregiver is likely to be admired and sought after. If you have found someone you really like, it's important that she know it. Increases in salary make us all feel valued (and able to keep up with the cost of living). You may want to give a slight raise after six months, but certainly, a raise should be given at the end of the first year.

Benefits

The specific benefits you will provide should be negotiated between you and the caregiver as part of your contract agreement. The following guidelines will help you in this process:

Sick days/personal days

All jobs should provide for some sick days with pay. Your caregiver won't be able to do a good job when she isn't well, and she shouldn't have to worry about a loss of pay. How many sick days you can offer is up to you, but for a twelve-month year, you should probably think in terms of at least six paid sick days.

Vacation

Just as you expect a vacation from your job, a full-time employee in your home needs one. Most common is one or two paid weeks at the end of the first year, and more for longer service. For many families it may be most convenient if the caregiver takes her vacation during the same period that you take yours. If you prefer this sort of arrangement, make sure to let her know well in advance, so she can make her plans accordingly.

If you would like the caregiver to accompany you on your family vacation, bear in mind that this is still work time for her and you need to arrange another time when she can take her own vacation.

You may need to be flexible, depending on the caregiver's circumstances. For instance, a young woman living in your house, far from her own family, might want to go home for the holidays, even if she has only worked for you for a few months. Discussing these issues in advance will help you avoid unplanned disruptions in your child's care and angry feelings between you and the caregiver.

Paid holidays

You and the caregiver should determine in advance which holidays will be taken with pay. The paid holidays you get from your own job will serve as a useful guide in this matter.

Medical insurance

Health benefits are important for anyone on any job, perhaps even more so for those working with young children, because they are frequently exposed to illness. If your caregiver does not have access to health coverage through a spouse or group plan, you may be able to get coverage for her by helping her join an organization that includes health plans for its members. The National Association for the Education of Young Children (NAEYC), an organization of early childhood professionals, parents, and others concerned with the welfare and education of young children, has such a plan (page 201).

Written Agreements

Drawing up a contract is usually helpful to both parents and caregivers. It gives you the opportunity to cover some of these issues and ensures that both parties are clear about the agreements they have made. The sample contract that follows can be modified to suit your specific situation.

SAMPLE CONTRACT FOR HOUSEHOLD EMPLOYMENT

Name of employee _____

Name of employer _____

Starting date: _____

Weekly hours: _____ Weekly salary: _____

Overtime rate: _____

Employee responsibilities: _____
_____
_____
_____

Employer-provided benefits:

Social Security _____

   Employer pays: _____ Employee pays: _____

Unemployment compensation _____

Workers' compensation _____

Disability insurance _____

Sick days _____ Vacation _____ Holidays _____

Weeks of termination notice required: _____

Employee's signature _____ Date _____

Employer's signature _____ Date _____

Beginning the Arrangement

If possible, hire the caregiver to begin on a part-time basis at least a week or two before you will actually need the care. During this time your child can get to know her gradually, in the security of your presence.

You also can use this time to familiarize the caregiver with your home or apartment and your daily routine. Make sure she knows how to use the oven, how the heating system works—in short, anything she needs to know to manage safely in your home. Be explicit in giving guidelines about safety, visitors, TV, and candy. Don't assume that her attitudes on these issues are the same as yours. Make sure to discuss *very specifically* what kinds of disciplinary methods are and are not acceptable to you. It isn't enough to say, "We don't spank our child," since the caregiver may not consider a swat on the hand or behind a spanking. Even if there are times when you yourself might think it's appropriate to spank your child, make it very clear that under no circumstances is physical punishment to be used, nor is harsh verbal punishment.

Take advantage of this time to get to know the caregiver better. She may have given you all the "right" answers to your questions, but now you can see how she acts with your child. How do you feel as you watch them together? Is the caregiver responsive to your child's needs? Is she following your instructions? Does your child seem to be relaxed around her? Do they seem to like each other?

When you feel ready to leave your child alone with the caregiver, begin the separation gradually. First just go out for a walk, do a few errands. Tell the caregiver and your child where you are going and when you will be back. Gradually increase the time spent away, until you are up to the hours that your arrangement will call for.

Make sure:

- to say goodbye directly to both your child and the caregiver. Never sneak away while your child is occupied, in order to try to avoid a scene. Separation feelings are natural, and your child and the caregiver need to work out a way to handle your departures.
- the caregiver knows if your child has a blanket, pacifier or toy for comfort and that she knows where to find it.
- to leave her, in addition to your own and your spouse's phone numbers, the names and numbers of your pediatrician and one or two

friends or relatives as emergency contacts. If you know neither you or your spouse will be reachable on a certain day, plan to call in at a specified time.

It is a good idea to post a form with emergency information right by your telephone. You can adapt the sample form opposite to your needs:

EMERGENCY INFORMATION

Child's name _____ Date of birth _____

Address _____ Apt. ____ Phone _____

Mother's name _____ Work phone _____ Ext. ____

Work address _____

Father's name _____ Work phone _____ Ext. ____

Work address _____

EMERGENCY CONTACTS:

Name _____ Relationship to family _____

Phone (days) _____ ext. ___ Phone (evenings) _____

Name _____ Relationship to family _____

Phone (days) _____ ext. ___ Phone (evenings) _____

Pediatrician _____ Phone _____ ext. ___

Address _____ Hospital affiliation _____

Closest hospital _____ Phone _____

Address _____

OTHER EMERGENCY NUMBERS:

Emergency number 911 (or your local code) _____

Poison control center _____ Fire department _____

Police precinct _____

CHILD'S HEALTH INFORMATION

Allergies _____

Special conditions _____

Current medications _____

EMERGENCY CONSENT FORM

I give consent for emergency medical treatment for my child

_____
Child's name

_____
Parent's signature   Date

In addition to posting this form at the phone, give a copy to the caregiver to keep in a small first-aid kit. This kit should go with her whenever she takes your child out. If any emergency occurs when she's not at your home, she will be able to reach you and/or the physician right away. It's a good idea to give the caregiver money for taxi fares and change for phone calls in case of an emergency.

Discuss guidelines for dealing with a variety of situations. Let the caregiver know specifically when you or your spouse should or should not be called at your job. For instance, if your child seems under the weather or cranky, even if there are no clear symptoms of illness, do you want her to call you? If your child gets hurt, throws up, is running a slight fever? Do not assume that she will know when it is appropriate to call—tell her exactly what you want. If your caregiver has not had any training in first aid, you may want to consider paying for her to take a course.

If the caregiver gets locked out, is there someone nearby with a key to your house? If you live in an apartment building, she should be introduced to the superintendent and know how to contact him if there is a problem in the apartment. If you live in a house, she should know your nearest neighbors.

In major emergencies, such as fires or serious injuries, make sure your caregiver knows the exact plan to follow—whom to contact and where to go. You cannot possibly anticipate all situations that may occur. One of the reasons for hiring this person should be a certain level of confidence that she would use good judgment when unexpected situations arise. To the extent that you can anticipate possible problems, however, you will both feel more at ease with a plan of action to follow.

Assessing the Arrangement

As your child and the caregiver become better acquainted, you can assess the arrangement more realistically. Even if you have been very careful in your selection, it is natural to wonder whether the particular person you have chosen is meeting your child's needs. If your child is already talking, he will probably tell you about what goes on when you're not there; with an infant or toddler, it's more difficult. However, if you plan to have some transition time in the morning and at the end of the day, you will be able to observe the relationship first hand.

Does the caregiver:

- respond to your child affectionately and with good humor?
- act in a manner that complements your own child-rearing methods?
- enjoy talking with you about your child's day?

Is she:

- arriving on time and ready to work?
- following your instructions about feeding, activities, etc.?
- getting to know your child's moods and signals?

Even if things seem to be going very well, it is not unusual to feel some anxiety in the early weeks of a new arrangement. There are a few things you can do to help relieve your worries.

One mother asked the caregiver to check in at a certain time:

During the first few months, I asked my caregiver to call me at work each day when Jessie was napping. That way I could hear about his morning and feel more in touch. It gave us a chance to chat too, and really made the separation easier.

- If you live in a city, ask a friend to go by the playground or park at a time when your child and the caregiver will be there. Have her visit with them and observe how they are doing. If you live in a suburban or rural area, ask a friend or relative to drop by your house at some point during the day to see how things are going.
- Come home at an unexpected time, just to see for yourself if all is as it should be. Ask your spouse to do the same.

Maintaining a Good Relationship

Most of us tend to start off a new arrangement by putting our best foot forward. You are likely to be very careful about not taking advantage of the caregiver, and she is likely to be punctual, enthusiastic and responsive. As time goes on, however, it's easy for both of you to take the arrangement for granted. Try to stay on top of the situation by sticking to the agreements you made:

- Make sure you come home when you are due, and have the caregiver's salary ready on time.
- Fill her in about changes in your child's behavior. If your baby had a bad night or isn't eating well, your preschooler is unusually cranky or fearful, or your older child is having trouble at school, it's important for her to know.
- Ask how things are going. Is she spending time with other caregivers and children? Does she have any questions? Are there places she might like to go with your child—a museum, library, park, beach, restaurant for lunch—for a break in the routine?
- Make sure to talk with her if you are making major changes such as weaning a baby from breast-feeding or starting on solid foods, cutting down on your toddler's bottles, or beginning toilet training. This way she will be attuned to possible reactions your child is having. Talk with the caregiver about how she can be supportive to you and your child during these transitions.
- If you are concerned about anything, bring it to her attention promptly. Be specific about your complaint and tell her what you expect. If she has a complaint or a suggestion about some change in your arrangements, pay attention to her concerns.
- Let her know that she is doing a good job and that you appreciate it.

It's also important to continue to watch how your child is reacting to the situation. Sometimes we are so grateful to have child care that we really don't want to know if something is not working well unless it's a major problem. If your child is verbal, talk with her about how she is feeling about the caregiver and how they are spending their time together. If you have an infant or toddler, pay attention to her mood when the caregiver is around. Most minor problems can be straightened out if you find out about them and deal with them directly.

If you have made a careful selection and followed these guidelines, your arrangement ought to work out well. There are, of course, situations in which problems arise that are not solvable and changes must be made. Even if all goes well, there will come a time when you will no longer need the services of the caregiver. When it is time to make a change, either planned or unexpected, there are ways to make the transition smoothly, with the least disruption and upset for you and your child. These matters will be addressed in Chapter 11.

5

Family Day Care

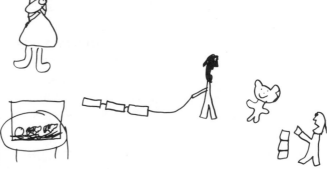

*F*amily day care is any ongoing arrangement in which your child is cared for in someone else's home. Long before it had a name, parents relied on this form of care, leaving their children with a neighbor down the street, a friend who was staying home with her own child, or a grandmother known in the neighborhood for providing child care.

In many parts of the country, family day care is the main source of care for infants and toddlers. In some areas, this type of care is used extensively for three- and four-year-old children as well. Family day care homes also provide care for school-age children, after school and during holidays and vacations. Many parents with unusual work schedules, or those who need occasional overnight care, have found that family day care gives them the most flexibility.

What Is Family Day Care Like?

There is tremendous variation in what you may see as you look at individual family day care homes. There are differences in the size of the group, the ages of the children, the style of the program and the qualifications of the providers. The following examples illustrate some of the diversity:

A mother has decided to stay home with her own young child. She is interested in caring for one or two other children, but she doesn't see herself as starting a long-term career as a child care provider. She is simply hoping to give her child some companionship, earn a little money, and offer a service to you as a parent. Basically, her days will be spent much the same way you would spend yours at home with your child. There will be time for play, small excursions to take care of errands at the bank or store, an outing to the park or playground, snacks and lunch, and a nap. She may have no specific equipment other than what is there for her own kids. She sees herself primarily as a mother who is extending her mothering to your child as well.

Such a program was started by this Atlanta mother when she couldn't find a satisfactory child care arrangement:

When my second child was born, after three months I suddenly had to go back to work. I tried to work part-time for three weeks taking the baby with me because I didn't want anyone else to take care of him except maybe my mother. I would drive eight or nine miles every morning to my mother's and then go back to the job. That lasted for three weeks and it was impossible for everybody. I couldn't find a solution and I decided the only thing I could do is to become a family day care provider myself. I've had to change everything completely around to make everything work but it means I can be home with my own children too.

A family day care provider has a small group program for five or six young children. She has been doing this type of work for some time and sees herself as having a career running a child care business. She may have formal training, or merely have acquired experience from years of practice. There is a planned program for the day, involving specific play activities, indoor and outdoor time, snacks and meals. She has allotted a specific room or rooms in her home or apartment for her business. She

has a variety of toys, books, and other equipment that she has selected specifically for her program.

Two or more providers, perhaps teachers trained in early childhood education, operate a group program for children of a specific age. (In some areas this is referred to as group family day care.) They consider themselves professionals and take time planning a well-balanced program for young children. Although their program is based in a home, it may be set up more like a nursery school, with cubbies, child-size tables and chairs, and specifically selected educational toys and equipment. There is a clearly stated educational philosophy to the program.

In this section, we will describe some of the factors you will need to consider in your search for family day care. Later in the chapter, there are guidelines for evaluating whether a particular family day care home is right for your child.

Size of Group

When you consider the size of the group, think about your child's age. How much adult attention does he require? If you have an infant or young toddler, would a group of six be too much for him? If you have a three- or four-year-old, would he benefit from a group experience? Think also about your child's temperament and the atmosphere that most suits it. Does your child feel overwhelmed when there are a lot of people around? Does he enjoy being in groups? Is your child able to ask adults for assistance or is he shy about expressing his needs? Would he feel comfortable in a busy, perhaps noisy environment with several other children and a lot of activity? Or would he be more relaxed in a calm and quiet atmosphere?

Age Range of the Group

There are some family day care providers who prefer to care for children of one age group, while others enjoy working with a mixed-age group. If you have an infant or toddler, you'll want to consider carefully not only the size of the group but the age range as well. Think about the kind of care an infant requires. Is it realistic to think that a single caregiver could do a good job alone with three or four infants? If, at the same time, two are hungry, another is cranky, and one is in the mood to play, clearly not all their needs can be met by a single person. On the other hand, the mix of one infant and a few older children can work out. Again, more than one infant, and neither age group is likely to get the attention it needs. Toddlers need the freedom to roam around, exploring their surroundings. Supervising two or three of them can be a challenge. Add more than one infant and the toddlers may end up spending more time in the playpen and the infants, more time in the crib.

For three- or four-year-olds, a group of peers may work out well. The design of the day can be geared to that age group, and your child will have others to play with. At this age, some children might find it boring to spend their days with much younger children.

There isn't a specific formula for what mix of ages will always work best. A great deal depends on the skill and experience of the provider. What is important is for you to consider exactly what your child needs and then determine whether that's possible within the age group a provider is serving.

This mother describes why she decided against a particular family day care home:

The woman I took my daughter to had two other children that were two years old and I was sort of worried about whether she could balance the needs of a six-month-old with a two-year-old. She was also uncomfortable because my daughter was very active. I thought it meant that she needed to control her, which I wasn't comfortable with. The trouble was that she knew the material on taking care of kids, but this was her first experience.

Qualifications of Providers

Family day care has attracted people from varying backgrounds and with a broad range of qualifications. A great many providers have chosen family day care as a career. They've taken training courses in child development, first aid, and business management. Some are experienced teachers who prefer to work in their own homes rather than in a school or day care center.

Not all caregivers, however, consider family day care a career or seek out specific training. A mother with a career in another field may see child care as temporary work while she stays home with her own young children. An older woman, who has raised her own family, may want to

care for one or two children in her home because she enjoys the work and needs to earn some money.

This mother found a good situation with such a provider:

Sandra has been staying three days a week with an older woman who is staying home. She is actually my neighbor across the street and it's perfect. She is very inexpensive and she really likes Sandra, and Sandra is the only child she is looking after.

In some instances, people who have had no *formal* training in the field may have acquired the skills necessary to do a good job. If you have an infant, for example, you might choose a woman who has lots of experience with babies—her own or other people's—and clearly handles them with a great deal of love, understanding, and skill even if she lacks formal training credentials.

Program

It is the family day care provider who sets the tone for what goes on in her home. Her feelings about children, her knowledge of how they develop, her sense of herself as a baby-sitter or professional child care provider will determine the way her program runs.

The degree of structure varies from home to home. A provider may follow the same routine every day—with playtimes, snacks, and outdoor activities occurring at specific times. She may be more flexible, varying routines from day to day. She may initiate and supervise many planned activities, like organized games or finger painting or gluing collages; or she may simply have toys available and let the children play as they like. A provider may plan activities with very specific expectations; for instance, she may cut certain shapes out of paper and ask everyone to make a house. Or she may have a more "child-centered" approach, encouraging each child to use materials in his own way. The caregiver's interests and skills will tend to guide what she does with the children. In some homes, for example, there may be a lot of cooking; in others, there may be an emphasis on music and dance or arts and crafts.

The differences you see may also reflect the ages of the children in care. It would not make sense to plan a busy day full of activities for infants. You should, however, expect to see varied materials and some planned activities for three- and four-year-olds.

Because space for day care centers is sometimes hard to find, some professional early childhood teachers are using their homes for the kind of preschool programs you might ordinarily expect to see in nursery schools or day care centers. In some areas these programs may be referred to as mini-centers. If you have a three- or four-year-old child and are considering this type of program, it will be helpful to read Chapter 7. The guidelines you will find there about program, equipment, and staffing would be applicable in these types of family day care homes as well.

The Caregiver's Style

We all have our personal styles and attitudes, and we relate to children and run our homes in our own way. It is the same with family day care providers. They may be comfortable being called by their first names or they may prefer Miss or Mrs. A caregiver may want to get to know you personally or wish to maintain a more formal relationship. There will be differences in how strict or lenient providers are about children's language, the level of noise that's permitted, table manners, and how much messy play is tolerated. Some homes are meticulously neat, others look more lived in. Choose the environment and style of care that's most compatible with your own.

Physical Environment

If a provider lives in a small apartment or home, she may have only one room available for the children to use. If she has more space, there may be separate areas for eating, playing, and napping. The home may look just like what it is, a home. Or the space may have been modified to be more like a playroom, with such things as lofts, small slides, and child-size tables and chairs.

The amount of space children have to play in and the freedom they have in using that space is important to large-muscle development and will also have an impact on how well the children relate to each other and the caregiver. Bigger and fancier, though, is not necessarily better. In evaluating the size of the physical space, consider the ages of the children, how many are in the group, whether the children seem too confined or seem to be enjoying themselves.

Although space is definitely an important consideration, the skill of the caregiver may compensate for a less than perfect physical layout, as this San Francisco mother found:

I saw some child care where the toys were nice and the atmosphere was nice but the providers didn't pay much attention. Then I went into a place that was a little more packed, the space was not quite as nice. But the person doing the care immediately sat down and talked to my daughter and gave her crayons and made contact with her before she paid any attention to me. I loved that, and that's who I chose.

Safety factors are vitally important. Proper ventilation, fire extinguishers and adequate exits, temperature control, toilet facilities, emergency procedures, and other health and safety factors are discussed later in this chapter.

Cost

The cost of family day care ranges from as little as $50 per week to as high as $250—for full-time care. Generally, a provider's rates will reflect the economic level of her neighborhood as well as how she sees herself and the work she is doing. Someone who thinks of herself as a babysitter is likely to charge less than someone who has training in the child care field and considers herself to be running a business. A licensed provider who is limited in the number of children she can have in her home may charge more than someone caring for a large, and possibly illegal, number of children. For you as a parent, child care costs may seem high, but it's important to remember that full-time care generally means the caregiver is caring for children ten hours a day. In many cases, her work hours are extended further by paperwork, consulting with parents, planning and shopping for meals, and keeping her home clean and safe for children.

Government Regulation

Although family day care has been the most common form of child care for a long time, it has remained largely unregulated by the government. There are currently over two hundred thousand providers nationwide who are part of their state's regulated systems. Experts in the field estimate that there are four to five times that number working outside of any regulated system.

Regulation is important because it sets standards for care in your community. It may bring providers out of isolation, linking them to valuable resources within the child care community. A regulated system may offer more opportunities for training, mutual support, access to equipment and liability insurance. Licensed family day care providers are eligible for the Child Care Food Program administered by the U.S. Department of Agriculture. (The food program provides reimbursement to providers for nutritious meals and snacks.)

Regulations won't guarantee that the care is of high quality or the style you prefer, but they can help you avoid some bad or unsafe conditions.

In those states where a license or certificate of some kind is now required to operate a family day care home, there is tremendous variation in the specific regulations: how many children can be cared for; what is considered a safe environment; what kind of inspections are required; and what qualifications a provider must meet. Even the terms for this process are not uniform. Providers may be *licensed, certified,* or *registered,* and these terms have differing definitions.

Depending on where a provider lives, she may be obliged to take training courses in first aid and child development or to attend a brief orientation session or perhaps no training whatsoever will be required. Some states have regulations for two different types of family day care homes—one for a small group of children and a single provider; the other, for a larger group and two or more providers.

Many family day care providers aren't aware that there are regulations regarding the care of children in the home. Others don't see any reason to become involved with governmental agencies because, even without licensing, they don't have any trouble finding parents who need their service. Some providers and parents resent the government's intrusion in what they consider a private arrangement—especially if they don't get much in return in the way of training, referrals, or equipment. Sometimes providers who try to get licensed find it a slow and difficult process. Regulatory agencies often have too few workers to carry out inspections and to process forms in a reasonable time.

Many parents now would prefer a licensed caregiver, but the reality is that you may have trouble finding one. Even if you are lucky enough to find a licensed provider, this is not an assurance of high quality care.

It is important to keep in mind that most public regulation seeks only to ensure that *minimum standards are being met*. In the end, it is up to you to thoroughly investigate before you choose a family day care home for your child.

This was vividly illustrated in one Minnesota community:

Whether a place is licensed doesn't always tell you the whole story. We sent Pat to a licensed family day care that was very close to where she went to school. But that woman often had twenty kids in her house and kids of all ages and it was pandemonium, a real mess. Clearly, she wasn't following the regulations. I couldn't believe it. Everybody in the neighborhood kept their kids there and it was an affluent neighborhood. But anyone who needed part-time care or drop-in care to go out to lunch, or even a full day, would use her. She was licensed, it was convenient, and she seemed pleasant. You trust those things when you probably should do a lot more investigating.

What Should the Guidelines and Requirements Be?

The National Association for Family Day Care (NAFDC), a professional membership organization representing family day care providers, offers the following guidelines as to what family day care regulations *should* include as minimum standards:

- A family day care home with one provider should have no more than six children, including the provider's own children. Within this group, not more than two of the children should be under the age of two.
- A group family day care home, with two or more providers, should have no more than twelve children, including the providers' own. Not more than four of the children should be under the age of two.
- A family day care provider should be *at least* eighteen years of age.
- He or she should have *at least basic training* in first aid, safety, and child development.

We have been discussing general guidelines of what you may expect to come across in your search for family day care. How, given all the variables, should you get started? What kind of choices should you make? What should you avoid? The following sections of this chapter have been designed to help you answer these questions.

Finding a Family Day Care Provider

An important first step is to check whether there is a child care resource and referral agency in your area. (Consult the directory on page 203.) If there is, call the local office and tell the staff what you are looking for. The counselors will be able to tell you about the regulation of family day care and what care is likely to cost. They will refer you to specific providers in your community and put you in touch with local family day care networks or associations that can give you the names of additional providers. CCRR groups are actively recruiting and training family day care providers and encouraging them to meet local regulatory requirements.

If you have difficulty locating a CCRR group where you live, contact the National Association of Child Care Resource and Referral Agencies (NACCRRA) for assistance (see page 248). The National Association for Family Day Care may also be able to provide you with resources and contacts in your area (see page 201).

What you have to choose from in family day care depends on where you live and the age of your child. This father expressed his frustration as he searched for infant care:

You would think that would be what they're for, but a lot of family day care providers really do not want to care for infants. That's partly because they live in walk-ups and that means dragging a stroller up the stairs, or they already have children that are two years old and it's easier just to take others the same age.

Your search may take a lot of time and energy. Try not to get discouraged. The more you get the word around, the better your chances are of finding the right situation for your child.

If you can't get the help you need from an organized group, you may want to try a few methods that have worked well for parents:

- Ask neighbors, friends, co-workers, and other parents in the area whether they know of anyone who offers family day care.
- Check with your pediatrician, obstetrician, pediatric clinic, or family doctor. Sometimes such people know of a mother staying home who would like to care for another child.
- Look for notices on bulletin boards at churches, synagogues, community centers, nursery schools, elementary schools, laundromats, day

care centers, health clinics, YMCAs, and libraries. Ask the people who work in these places whether they know of people who provide family day care.

- Post your own notices in these places.
- Run a classified ad, seeking family day care, in a local community paper.
- If you are near a university or college, advertise in its paper.

Screen Potential Caregivers by Phone

Once you have the names of some potential providers, you can save time and trouble by doing your initial screening over the telephone. Ask the provider right away if it's a convenient time for her to talk. If she is caring for children, she can't and shouldn't spend time in lengthy phone conversations, as this parent quickly realized:

Now that I am looking for part-time child care, I have been calling some people. My sense is that to call them during the day is really difficult because they're so busy. They really don't have time to spend telling you about what they do. It can be kind of unsettling. . . . I remember calling a couple of people and I could hear babies really crying in the background, which probably doesn't mean anything except when you are worried about looking for child care and then you hear a baby screaming . . .

Use a work sheet like the one that follows to jot down basic information:

PROVIDER SCREENING SHEET

Date Called: _____

Name: _____ Phone: _____

Location _____

Hours/days available: _____

Number of children cared for: _____

Ages of children: _____

Fees: _____

Licensed?   yes _____   no _____   In process _____   Not applicable _____

Additional comments: _____

_____

_____

Bear in mind that providers are also screening you, wanting to find out if yours is a family they want to deal with. Some providers prefer not to discuss specifics of placement or fees until you have met in person. They may suggest that you visit first and then explore whether an arrangement can be worked out. Obviously, if you are speaking with several people, it will be easier if you can get enough information to help you decide if a visit makes sense. But it's important to remember that you are a stranger to the provider and she simply may not feel comfortable giving you a great deal of information about her home and family at this early stage. You will have to play it by ear. If the provider seems amenable to discussing her program over the phone, go ahead and ask your questions. If not, save them for your meeting.

Some things you should find out are:

- How long has she been caring for children in her home?
- How many children is she currently caring for? What are their ages?
- How large is her house or apartment? How much space is used by the children?
- Does she have her own children? What are their ages? Are they home during the day?
- Has she had any training in child development? First aid?
- Is she affiliated with any agency or group of family day care providers?
- Is she licensed?
- Does she work alone or have an assistant?
- What does she do for backup if she or her child gets sick?

If you are feeling favorably impressed by her responses, ask her if you can have the names of two parents who are currently using her care or have recently used it, so you can call them for references. Some providers may not feel comfortable about involving other parents unless you are ready to seriously consider using the care. They may suggest you visit first. *The important thing is to make sure you check references before you commit your child to anyone's care.*

Checking References

When you call other parents to ask about a family day care provider, listen to the tone of voice they use as well as what is actually said. Are their responses flat or enthusiastic? Do they seem uncomfortable about being asked to be a reference? Do they hesitate as they answer your questions? Often people don't like to give negative references unless their experiences were really dreadful. Asking specific questions about their experiences might help you elicit the information you want:

- How long has your child been in the home?
- How does your child feel about the caregiver?
- What do you particularly like about the program and provider?
- Is there anything you don't like about the care your child receives?
- Do you find the caregiver easy to talk to?

Visiting a Family Day Care Home

It is absolutely essential that you visit any family day care home you are considering. Caregivers who sound like good possibilities over the phone may turn out to be unacceptable when you meet them in person and see the environment they've created. As this mother describes:

When I had to find somebody new to take care of my son, I put an ad in the local paper and got hundreds and hundreds of phone calls from people who wanted to do it. I did some screening over the phone and then I went and met with people and it was very depressing. People lived in extremely small apartments, had more children than I would feel comfortable with, and their apartments weren't clean. It felt like I could never leave my child in this kind of setting. Toys were put away in boxes and they had to be pulled out, and then when they did, it was like the whole floor looked like a sea of toys.

Sometimes, just the opposite happens. This mother felt full of doubts after her initial phone conversation with the provider, but since her choices were limited, she went to meet her:

The first time I called the woman who takes care of my son, when she told me where she lived—it's this big, ugly two-story house—I thought, Well, this one is going to be a little strange. Also, she has an accent. It isn't really hard to understand her, but on the phone, especially the first time you talk to her . . . Well, I was unsure about her. I didn't have that much choice, but I put her low on my list. Now, I am glad I went ahead because it worked out fine.

Since you may be visiting several places, it is best not to involve your child until you think you have found a home that is a real possibility. Then, arrange a time when you can bring your child to meet the caregiver before you make a final decision. This initial visit will give you the opportunity to meet the provider and see whether you feel the home would be a good place for your child. We will discuss the criteria point by point, but the general goal of this visit is to give you the chance to:

- observe the caregiver working with children.
- explore the safety and physical set-up of the day care home.
- talk with the caregiver about her feelings on child care in general and about your child's care in particular.

If the provider is currently caring for other children, try to schedule your visit so that you will be able to see parents and children either arriving in the morning or leaving in the afternoon. This will give you a glimpse of how the parents and caregiver relate to one another and how well the caregiver helps families make the transition between home and child care.

During your visit, try to stay in the background and observe what's going on. Tell the caregiver that you understand she needs to focus her attention on the children, doing what she normally does. If you like what you see, schedule another visit for a time when the children are napping or after they go home, when the two of you will be able to talk in depth.

Explore the Family Day Care Home

This is your opportunity to check thoroughly on the physical aspects of the family day care home:

- Is the home clean and in good repair?
- Are there good light and ventilation?
- Are there safety guards on the windows?
- Are there smoke detectors?
- Are there fire extinguishers?
- Is there more than one way out in case of fire?
- Are there covers on electrical sockets?
- Are there radiator covers?
- If there are stairs, are there safety gates?
- If there are pets, are they clean, healthy, and friendly?

Ask the provider to show you what areas of the house or apartment are used for the child care program. Is there enough space for children to play? Are the furniture and equipment appropriate for their age and size? If the children take naps, find out where and on what. Find out where the caregiver stores medicines and household products that could be harmful to children. Ask if she has a good first-aid kit available.

Ask to see the kitchen. Is it clean? Does the food seem fresh? Is it well stored? Are there flies, roaches, or evidence of mice? Are knives and other dangerous utensils and cleaning supplies out of the children's reach?

Ask to see the bathroom the children use. Is it clean? Are there potties? Is there a step stool for children to reach the sink? Does each child have an individual towel, or are there disposable towels?

If the provider cares for infants or toddlers, ask to see the diaper-changing area. Are fresh pads or papers used whenever a baby is changed. Is there a safety belt on the changing table? Are the wipes, diapers, and other supplies all within the caregiver's reach while she changes the baby?

You may feel uncomfortable inspecting another person's home so carefully, but an experienced provider will be familiar with parent visits and should encourage you to explore her home thoroughly. New providers may feel more nervous about your visit. Make allowances for their inexperience.

Examine the Equipment

The kind of equipment a caregiver has usually depends on how many children she cares for and their ages. If there are infants or toddlers, are there cribs? Are they clean and sturdy? Are there bumper guards? Are the mattresses in good shape? Are there high chairs and infant seats with safety belts? Are there toys and books that are safe for children to put in their mouths? If the provider has preschool children in her care, are there books appropriate to their age level? Is there a variety of play materials available—crayons, scissors, paper, paints, balls, blocks, cars and trucks, puzzles, dolls? Is the equipment in good shape? Is it arranged so that it's appealing and accessible to the children?

Inspect the Outdoor Play Space

Ask to see the outdoor play space the children use. If the provider lives in an apartment, ask where she takes the children to play outdoors. If she has more than one or two children in her care, ask her how she gets back and forth from the playground or park and what her plan is if there is an emergency or a child gets injured. Go with her, or go later on your own, to look at the outdoor facilities.

- Is the play area in a safe place?
- Is the equipment in good condition?
- Is the play area well fenced?
- Is the surface grass, rubber, or sand?
- Is the area laid out so that every child can be seen?

If the caregiver has her own yard, check the following:

- Is the play area defined by thick bushes or fencing so children cannot wander off?
- Is it well protected from roads and driveways?
- If there is a pool, pond, or stream, is it totally inaccessible to the children without adult assistance?
- If there are swings, slides, and other equipment, are they in good condition? Is there enough equipment for the number of children in the home?
- Is the area free of sharp rocks, ditches, or other hazards?

Observing the Program

When you look at the activities that take place in the home, think about your child's age and current stage of development. Try also to think ahead a bit, particularly if you have an infant. Within months, your baby will be an active toddler.

Here are some general guidelines of what you *should* and *should not* see, regardless of the age of the children in care:

You should see children who:
- seem to feel comfortable in the home, free to touch things, and move about the way they would in your own home.
- are happily occupied with activities and each other.
- approach the caregiver easily when they need her help or attention.
- request food when they're hungry and see the food served to them in an appetizing manner. There should be some flexibility about snacks

and mealtimes, particularly for very young children, who may ask for juice or snacks frequently and not be able to wait for a designated time.
- need their diapers changed responded to promptly. The caregiver should wash her hands after every diaper change. Young children learning to use the potty or toilet should be able to do so whenever they need to and be assisted cheerfully by the caregiver. If a child soils her clothes, this should be handled calmly, without embarrassing the child. The caregiver should make sure children wash their hands after using the toilet.

You should see caregivers who:
- help young children find enjoyable activities.
- talk and play directly with the children.
- respond promptly if a child is in distress or has a question or a problem.
- resolve disputes between children fairly and calmly.

You should see a schedule that includes:
- active play, such as dancing, building with big blocks, playing outdoors.
- quiet play, such as looking at books, drawing, pasting, playing with manipulative toys.
- a nap or a quiet resting period, depending on the ages and needs of the children.
- snacks and meals.

You should NOT see:
- children left unsupervised, even briefly.
- children running randomly around the house or apartment.
- children sitting quietly because there is nothing to do.
- children hurting each other, with no adult intervention.
- toys that are inaccessible to the children, unsafe, or not appropriate for their ages.
- food used either as a bribe or punishment.
- candy, soda, and other sweets used as snacks—unless it is a special party of some kind.
- food that can cause choking in children under three: *raw* carrots, grapes, peanuts, hot dogs (unless they are skinless), popcorn, hard

sucking candies or honey (which can cause respiratory failure in infants). The caregiver may not know that such foods are dangerous. If she is serving them, tell her they pose a potential hazard.

- any physical discipline *at all*, under any circumstances, by a caregiver to a child. This includes hitting, shaking, yanking children by their arms, or putting them in any kind of restriction. Even if there are some circumstance in which you might spank your own child, no one else should use any physical discipline.

- children isolated as punishment—sent to another room, put in a chair facing the wall, stood in a corner, told to sit in a cubby. Sometimes a child who is having a difficult time and hurting other children may need a time-out, where she can sit quietly for a little while doing a project by herself. However, the child should remain part of the group, able to see and hear the caregiver and her peers.

- any aspect of the children's physical privacy being impinged on by adults. Although young children generally need and enjoy physical contact with adults, it's important to notice who initiates the contact and when. You should not see caregivers continue to tickle, hug, or kiss children who are obviously uncomfortable and trying to wriggle away. Caregivers should not insist on being kissed hello or goodbye.

- any verbal reprimand that shames or embarrasses a child in front of his peers or any excessively loud shouting. Notice whether the caregiver differentiates between the child's behavior and the child when she is scolding. "Johnny, you may not hit. It hurts and we don't allow it here" is appropriate. "Johnny, you are a bad boy who doesn't know how to play" is not.

Talk with the Provider in Depth

Before you talk with the provider, make a list of the questions you want to ask. Take notes during your visit. If you didn't understand something about the way the caregiver handled a particular situation, discuss it with her in your meeting. Consider carefully your own child's style, likes, and dislikes so that you can ask specific questions about what his day would be like. Does the provider seem to have a good grasp of what's appropriate for someone of your child's age?

If you really want to understand the caregiver's attitudes about children and child rearing, ask open-ended questions so that she won't tailor her responses to what she thinks you want to hear.

If you have an infant, some general questions you might ask, are:

- How often does she think infants should be fed?
- When do the babies' diapers get changed?
- How long would she let a baby cry before picking him up?
- What does she think a baby needs from a caregiver at this age?
- Does she think babies get "spoiled" if they are held too much?

Then ask specific questions about what's on your mind about your own baby. For instance, if you've been nursing, ask how she thinks you should handle the transition to the bottle. If your baby is used to two long naps a day, ask if the caregiver would be able to follow this routine. If your child uses a pacifier, ask what she thinks about it.

The caregiver's responses to these questions are important, but she should also ask you how *you* feel about these issues. The heart of your relationship, if it is to be a good one, will depend on communication of this sort. Her ways of handling your baby may not turn out to be exactly the same as yours. That may be fine as long as it is a style that works well with your baby and is acceptable to you.

If you have a toddler or a two-year-old, some general questions you might ask are:

- How does she handle it when a child says no and refuses to do what she asks?
- What activities does she enjoy doing with toddlers?
- What kind of outdoor play does she think children of this age need?
- How does mealtime work? Are the children fed or encouraged to feed themselves? How does she feel if things get messy?
- When does she think is the best time to begin toilet training? How does she think it should be introduced?
- How does she feel about bottles? Pacifiers? Security blankets and stuffed animals? Does she limit their use, or are they available to the children whenever they want them?

Then, talk specifically about issues you are facing with your own child and ask her how she thinks they should be handled. For instance: If your child is trying to use a cup but keeps spilling, would she encourage him or give him a bottle? If he's used to lullabies at nap time, would she sing to him? This is the first time you are going to be separated from him; what does she suggest to make it easier for both of you?

If you have a three- or four-year-old, some general questions you might ask are:

- What skills does she think children of this age should be developing?
- What kinds of activities does she plan for them?
- Does she think it's important to read to children? What are some of her favorite children's books for this age group?
- How does she handle it if a child misbehaves or does not follow her instructions?
- If there is a large group of children, are they all expected to conform to certain routines? How much flexibility is there for individual children?

Then, think about your child and ask what is on your mind. For instance: If your child is shy around other children, how will she help him make friends? You've noticed your son is particularly interested in music; does she have instruments in the home? You had another baby recently; will your child feel pushed out by starting day care now? Does she have suggestions from her experience that will help you explain it to him?

If you have a school-age child who will be in the family day care home for part of the day and also on days when there is no school, some general questions you might ask are:

- What kinds of games and activities are available?
- Does she expect the older children to help with the younger ones, or do they play on their own?
- Does she provide an after-school snack?
- What does she think a child most needs after a day at school?
- Does she supervise the children's homework?
- Are older children allowed to play in the yard, road, or street? What kind of supervision is there?

Think about what your child would want to do if he or she was coming home directly from school. Discuss this picture with the caregiver to see if the day can be similar in her home. Does she have games that involve winners and losers? How does she handle the children's feelings in these situations? Does she expect the children to have a quiet time after school or to run around? Can the children do their homework if they want to?

If a provider is working with children of several ages, ask her how she accommodates their differing needs. Think about how your child would fit in with the other children and whether she would be overwhelmed or happily stimulated.

Since you may be visiting several homes, it may be helpful to take the checklist on page 76 with you so you can record your reactions.

FAMILY DAY CARE CHECKLIST

Name of provider: _____

Address: _____

Date: _____

BASIC INFORMATION	Yes	No
Program licensed	___	___
Hours acceptable	___	___
Fees affordable	___	___

GENERAL ATMOSPHERE	Yes	No
Home safe and well maintained	___	___
Setting cheerful	___	___
Toys safe and appropriate	___	___
Good light and ventilation	___	___
Smoke detectors, fire extinguishers	___	___
Medicines/household products locked away	___	___

CAREGIVERS	Yes	No
Seem to enjoy children	___	___
Respond quickly to children's needs	___	___
Play with children	___	___
Gentle in handling children	___	___

THE PROGRAM	Yes	No
Activities are varied and age-appropriate	___	___
Children play outdoors each day	___	___
There is a clear schedule for meals, naps, playtimes	___	___

PARENT INVOLVEMENT	Yes	No
Parents are welcome to spend time in the home	___	___
Parents meet with caregiver on a regular basis	___	___

GENERAL REACTIONS

Thinking It Over

Now that you have gathered a fair amount of information, consider these questions in making your decision. There are no perfect care situations. Your goal is to make the best arrangement possible for your child.

- Is the home safe?
- Are the caregiver's attitudes toward children compatible with or complementary to your own?
- Is the caregiver's style appropriate for your child's age and temperament?
- Would the size of the group allow your child to get the attention she needs?
- Would the activities be enjoyable?
- If there is a disagreement, would you be comfortable discussing it with the caregiver?

Have you asked all your questions? Have they been answered satisfactorily?

Making Your Decision

Think about what you have seen and heard and then add another ingredient to your considerations: How do you *feel* about the home and the provider? This midwestern father went directly to the heart of the matter:

We had a hard time choosing between two good caregivers. I think the thing that really pushed us to Sylvia was that when she was talking to us, she would take time out and address the kids directly. It was real evidence that they were having a good time. The other thing is that a friend of ours had her child there. I met her in the grocery store and she couldn't say enough good things about Sylvia. That was important, but the key thing was how much those kids enjoyed the woman that was going to be their caregiver. We felt she could love our children a lot.

If the situation feels right to you, take that reaction seriously. If you have *any* uneasy feelings about the family day care home or the provider, look elsewhere. You do not have to find objective reasons for your feelings. You are the best judge of what your child needs. Bear in mind that if you feel you have made a mistake, your decision can be changed. Over the first few weeks your child is in the home, you can watch carefully and evaluate your choice.

When you do feel that you have found a good situation for your child, the next step is to formalize the agreement so you can get started.

Written Agreements

It is important to have a clear written agreement with the provider about what you both expect. Good family day care requires open communication between parents and caregiver. The more explicit you are with one another, the less likely you will be to run into misunderstandings that might disrupt your child's care. Many family day care providers have their own well thought out contracts and well-organized systems. If the particular provider you choose does not have such forms, you can go over the points covered on the following pages and modify the sample forms to fit your particular situation.

These are some of the issues that you should make sure are discussed and written down so you are both clear that you are operating with the same understanding:

- The specific days and hours that the caregiver will take care of your child.
- Her fees and payment policies. Will she expect to be paid weekly? Monthly? By check? In cash? How much notice will she give you if she is raising her fees? In order to claim the Child Care Tax Credit offered by the Internal Revenue Service, you will need to have receipts and the caregiver's Social Security number. Find out if this is acceptable to her.
- Will you be required to pay if your child is out with a brief illness? A long illness? When you are on vacation? Be specific about the number of days involved.
- Her overtime policies and charges.
- Her arrangement about food. Does she provide it? What kind of food does she serve? Can you make suggestions? If you are to provide it, what are you to send? Full meals, including beverage? Snacks?

- Are you supposed to supply diapers, or are they included in your fee?
- Her vacation and holiday schedule. How much notice will you have if there are changes in the schedule?
- Her emergency backup plan. Does she have another adult on call? Can you meet this person? What is her phone number? Will you be notified if she changes her backup person? Does she have contact with a local doctor?
- Her policy about illness. Under what circumstances would she expect you to keep your child home or pick him up early if he got sick?
- How much notification will she give you if she is closing her program or asking you to leave for any other reason?
- How much notification must you give her if you are removing your child from the program?

SAMPLE PARENT/PROVIDER AGREEMENT

Provider _____

Parent _____

Child _____

Days and hours of care _____

Payment policies:

Fee _____ Payments due (weekly, monthly, etc.) _____

Overtime _____ If child is absent _____

Parent will provide: _____

_____

_____

Caregiver will provide: _____

_____

_____

Substitute caregiver:

Name: _____

Address: _____ Phone: _____

Holidays/vacations (no care provided) _____

_____

Amount of termination notice required:

From parent _____ From provider _____

Parent's signature: _____ Date _____

Provider's signature: _____ Date _____

Emergency Information

Make sure the caregiver has the following information in writing about you and your child *before* you ever leave the child in her care, even briefly.

- You and your spouse's full name, address, and home phone number.
- The work address, phone number, title, and schedule of both parents.
- The name, address, and phone number of your pediatrician, health center or family doctor, and their hospital affiliations.
- At least two emergency contacts: relatives, friends, or neighbors who can be called if you are unreachable.
- The names, *in writing*, of any people other than you or your spouse who have permission to pick up your child. Make sure you tell the caregiver exactly how you will notify her if there is any change in your usual pickup arrangement.
- Make sure the caregiver has appropriate medical information about your child—i.e., allergies, special conditions, or any medications your child is taking.

EMERGENCY INFORMATION

Child's name _____ Date of birth _____

Address _____ Apt. ____ Phone _____

Mother's name _____ Work phone _____ ext. ____

Work address _____

Father's name _____ Work phone _____ ext. ____

Work address _____

Persons authorized to pick up my child:

Name _____ phone _____

Name _____ phone _____

Emergency contacts:

Name _____ Relationship to family _____

Phone (days) _____ (evenings) _____

Name _____ Relationship to family _____

Phone (days) _____ (evenings) _____

Pediatrician _____ Phone _____ ext. ____

Address _____ Hospital affiliation _____

Child's health information:

Allergies _____

Special conditions _____

Current medications _____

I give consent for emergency medical treatment for my child

_____
Name of child

_____
Parent's signature   Date

Getting Started

Sometimes children take a long time to adjust to going off to day care, as this mother found:

My daughter couldn't express that she didn't like the idea that I was working outside the home and she was going to day care. She complained about the way the lady made macaroni and cheese. It wasn't the way Mom made it! I kept addressing the little things, trying to straighten them out, not being able to see what the big issue was with her. The next fall, I took her to a different day care home and she had a different complaint—that the other kids all knew each other and she was an outsider. The following year, we tried yet another day care home and that one worked out very well. I think it wasn't that the provider was better than the other ones. It was just that my daughter had finally accepted the fact that Mom was working outside the home and she went to day care.

There are ways to smooth the transition so that your child will make a happy adjustment to child care. Children need to know exactly what is being planned for them. If your child is old enough to understand, talk about the family day care home and take her to visit before the day your arrangement will begin. Don't, though, overload a child under two with more information than she can handle. Take her for a visit and then, the day before she will be starting, tell her that you will be going back to Mrs. Smith's house to play. The child needs to get to know the provider and feel comfortable in the home before the idea of staying without you will have any meaning.

On the way to the home, tell your child how much time you will both stay: "until lunch time"; or, "when it's time for your nap." If your child is three or four years old, she will remember her visit. Talk about what her days will be like, as concretely as possible: "I will take you there every morning after we have breakfast. You will be able to play with those blocks you liked. Mrs. Smith will take you to the park. After lunch you will have a rest and play some more. Daddy will pick you up every day, and I will see you when you get home." Let her know that you will be staying with her for a while, while she gets to know the other children and the caregiver. If your child has questions, answer them honestly. If you are not sure of an answer, tell her you will make sure to ask Mrs. Smith about it.

Discuss with the caregiver the best way to begin the arrangement.

Definitely plan to spend some time with your child in the day care home before you leave her there. You may want to bring the child for a brief period of time each day for several days before extending to longer care. How many days you should stay will depend on your child's age, previous care experiences, general adjustment patterns, and how much time you can take if you are working. You and the caregiver will need to decide together on a good plan.

After the initial phasing-in period, you should always be able to have access to your child at any time. One referral agency staff member described a situation that was totally inappropriate:

I got a call from one woman, who said a provider told her they couldn't come to visit after their son started. They would have to leave the child at the door. I told her she had the right to come in to visit and drop in anytime and that she shouldn't leave her child in a house like that.

The first time you plan to leave, whether it's after a day, a few days, or a week, make sure that both the caregiver and your child know you will be leaving. Even if it will only be for a brief period, tell the caregiver and your child the exact plan. Since young children do not have a clear conception of time, be very concrete in your explanation. For instance: "I will come back after you finish your lunch." Or, "When it is time to listen to stories, I will come back."

When you are ready to begin your regular care schedule, you can help ease your child's adjustment by:

- talking with the caregiver about how your child generally adjusts to new situations.
- making sure the caregiver knows if your child has a special object for security—a blanket, a doll—and being sure it's available.
- giving your child a photograph of you to keep with her.
- letting your child bring some small object of yours—a scarf, a set of keys—to the day care home.
- telephoning at an agreed upon time of day to check in and saying hello to your child—if she is old enough and the caregiver thinks it will not be disruptive.
- coming back exactly when you said you would.

Most important: Never leave your child at the home without clearly saying goodbye to the caregiver and the child. It may be tempting to "sneak off" while your child is involved in play, but it will leave him very distrustful of the arrangement. He may feel sad and cry when you leave. This is a natural reaction to separation. If you and the caregiver feel that the child has had enough time to adapt to the new situation, trust the caregiver to support him through the sad feelings and get him involved in activities. To reassure yourself, call a little later to make sure he is feeling better.

Assessing the Arrangement

As your child and the caregiver become better acquainted, you can assess the relationship more realistically. Even if you have been very careful in your selection of a family day care home, it is natural to wonder whether you've made the right decision.

As you observe the developing relationship between the caregiver, your child, and the other children in the group, here are some things to notice.

Does your child:
- respond to the caregiver warmly when you arrive in the morning?
- settle into play easily with a favorite toy or a new friend?
- show you or tell you about the day's activities?

Do you as a parent:
- feel comfortable spending time in the home?
- find the caregiver responsive to your comments and suggestions?
- feel that your instructions are being followed?

Nurturing the Family Day Care Relationship

Family day care works best when parents and caregiver work as partners in considering the child's needs. There are several ways in which you as a parent can contribute to helping this relationship flourish.

- Keep to the agreements you have made. Don't take advantage of the caregiver's time and good nature by arriving earlier in the morning or later in the evening than arranged.

- Plan on a few minutes of transition time in the morning and at pickup time so you can exchange relevant information on matters like what your child's had to eat, whether she slept well or was cranky or had a great day.
- Set aside time once a month for a detailed talk about how things are going.
- If you are concerned about something, bring it to the caregiver's attention promptly. Ask her when would be a good time to have a talk (unless it's a safety matter requiring immediate attention). When you do talk, be specific about your complaint or question.

There are times when you should discuss a problem immediately—as this Minnesota mother found:

My son was in a licensed family day care home and I gave them a car seat that he has to use in the car. But then one day I went early to get him. They were just coming back from Burger King and I saw my son on the backseat with a seat belt on but no car seat. None of the kids had car seats. I confronted the provider right there, and she said, "Well, we just left in a hurry today." My husband and I went to see her the next morning and insisted the car seat be used from then on.

Your child will appreciate links between the family day care home and his own:

- Ask the caregiver if you can cook something with your child that he can bring to share with his friends.
- Ask if you can spend a morning or afternoon in the home helping out or go with the group on a trip.
- Invite the caregiver to your home to see your child's room or share a meal.
- Ask the caregiver if she would like you to collect materials like egg cartons, shoe boxes, or fabric scraps that can be used for art activities.

Your Child's Adjustment

Individual children react to separation in different ways. A child may cry during the first few days of the arrangement and then seem to adjust happily; she may bounce off quite cheerfully almost immediately and later, perhaps in a few days or weeks, have trouble saying goodbye when you leave. Your child may not want to leave the day care home when you arrive, as if to say, "I had to wait for you, now you wait for me." She may be fine in the day care home but give you trouble in the evening. Some children flourish from the beginning and never seem to have difficulty handling the separation.

This woman saw the situation from the caregiver's point of view:

When I was doing family day care, I watched how the separation always seemed to be worse for the parent than for the child. The child might cry when Mom left, but by the time she was on the street, the kid would stop crying and be part of the gang. Sometimes I would tell the parents, "When you get to work, call me and I'll let you know what's going on." Sometimes I've even noticed that at five o'clock, when the mother came to pick up that same crying kid, he would say, "I'm not ready to go home. I want to stay and play some more."

You and the caregiver should be discussing your child's reactions as you go along. If you have made a careful selection and work closely with the caregiver, things are likely to work out well. There are situations, however, where for one reason or another a child will simply not be happy in the home you've selected. There may also be a situation in which the provider decides to discontinue her program and you are forced to find other arrangements. Or you may develop problems in your relationship with the caregiver that are hard to predict:

Something you wouldn't think about but that's tricky with family day care . . . the caregiver welcomed me into her house like a friend. You know, "Just go put the milk into the refrigerator, feel free to do this, do that." And then I think, over time, she realized that she needed boundaries. She was sort of saying, through her actions, I think we have to step back and try to do this again. But by that time both of us realized that it was really too late—too many awkward things had gone on between us.

Even if all goes smoothly, there will come a time to end the arrangement. Making changes in child care arrangements involves feelings for both you and your child. In Chapter 11, we will discuss how to handle these transitions.

6

Infant/Toddler Centers

*I*nfant/toddler centers provide group care for very young children. Although this type of care is quite common in other countries, it has been slow to develop in the United States. One reason is the high cost of providing care for such young children. More caregivers are needed per child than are necessary with older age groups. Many of the agencies that operate centers for preschool children simply cannot afford to do so for infants and toddlers.

Economics, however, is only one of the factors that has affected the slow development of this type of child care. Our society has been resistant to the *idea* of institutionalized settings for the care of little babies. We imagine rooms crowded with cribs or little toddlers lined up in rows of high chairs. That seems much too regimented and cold an atmosphere to most Americans, who seem to prefer that infants and toddlers be with a caregiver in their own home or in the provider's. This California mother expressed her real fears about infant-center care:

It was my first time using child care, and my child was, like, four months old. I heard so many rumors about how child care was and saw these articles and television interviews about people who got caught doing things devious with kids and it really scared me. So I got into this program—an infant center—instead of going to my school. I was basically there all day watching the kids, watching the workers, and making sure that my child was well kept. I was trying to work my classes around where I could still be there almost all day till I really got to know the individuals. There was no way I was just going to drop my baby off.

Attitudes are changing, though. Research seems to show that it is not the *setting* of care that matters as much as the *quality* of that care. Well-designed centers can create an atmosphere that is warm, supportive, and very much like a home.

In the next few years, infant/toddler centers are likely to be opening up at a more rapid pace. There is simply not enough in-home care and family day care available to meet the growing demand for care of children under the age of three.

What is Quality Care in an Infant/Toddler Center?

We've learned a lot about what the key elements are in quality care in a center setting. Good programs will have small groups of children, with enough adults to give a great deal of individual attention to infants and toddlers. This adult-child ratio is crucial. The staff should be knowledgeable about the way young children develop and skilled in handling them. The same caregivers ought to be with the group each day so that young children can form attachments to individual adults. The plan of the day should revolve around the individual tempos and temperaments of the children. You shouldn't see the precise scheduling of play periods, snacks, and naps that work with older children. Instead, there should be the flexibility to take into account the different needs of each young child in the group. Equally important, a good center will encourage a partnership between parents and staff, with open and ongoing communication.

Government Regulation

The National Association for the Education of Young Children (NAEYC), a professional membership organization of teachers, parents, and others concerned with the healthy growth and development of young children, has made the following recommendations for group size and staff-child ratios:

- For infants (birth to one year) groups with a *maximum* of eight infants and two caregivers—a staff-child ratio of 1:4.
- For toddlers (twelve to twenty-four months) a *maximum* group size of twelve children, with three caregivers—a staff-child ratio of 1:4.
- For two-year-olds (twenty-four to thirty-six months) a *maximum* group size of twelve children, with two caregivers—a staff-child ratio of 1:6.

These are *minimum* standards. A higher ratio of adults to children, particularly where infants and toddlers are concerned, is always preferable.

Unfortunately, government regulation of infant/toddler centers has thus far done little toward ensuring quality care. Many states have set *no* limitations on group size. Even where there are some standards, they vary alarmingly, with some states allowing for as many as eight babies with one caregiver.

Few states have set requirements for the qualifications of staff who work with infants and toddlers. Even where relatively good standards have been set for teachers at the preschool level, there are generally only minimal requirements for people who work with the youngest children.

The fact that licensing standards are so poor makes your search for good care much harder. You must really know what to look for and what to avoid. The following sections will first give you "the lay of the land" —what you may see as you look around at infant/toddler centers. Then you will find the specifics: how to locate and judge individual programs.

What Are Infant/Toddler Centers Like?

What Ages Are Served?

Although some programs accept infants as young as six weeks old, it is more common for centers to take children at either three or six months of age and provide care until the child is three years old. If the program is part of a larger preschool center, care may continue through kindergarten age. In some programs, infants and toddlers may be grouped together; in others, there are separate rooms and separate staff members for each age group. One arrangement is not necessarily better than the other. It depends on the total size of the group, the adult-child ratio, and the skill of the caregivers.

In a mixed-age group, it is important that the staff be responsive to the differing needs of the children. For instance, infants might need several naps a day, whereas some toddlers may need one nap and a two-year-old may have given up napping completely. Some infants will still be using bottles exclusively, while others have started eating solid food. Although two-year-olds are generally able to make themselves understood even with a very limited vocabulary, infants are still totally dependent on the caregiver's ability to discern their needs.

What Hours of Care Are Provided?

Though some centers offer only part-day programs, with children attending either morning or afternoon sessions, many programs are specifically designed to meet the needs of working parents and offer a full day of care. The exact hours may vary depending on where you live. In some parts of the country, for instance, full-time care generally means from 8:00 A.M. to 6:00 P.M. In other areas, many centers are open from 6:00 A.M. to 6:00 P.M.

Who Operates the Centers?

Many infant/toddler centers are run as nonprofit programs, sponsored by churches, synagogues, community organizations, or YMCAs. Some are affiliated with graduate programs in education. There are, however, an increasing number of centers that are run as profit-making enterprises. They may be small mom-and-pop operations or centers run either by local companies or by large corporations that license franchises around the country.

Who Staffs the Programs?

Because there is so little in the way of government regulation, you may see quite a range in the knowledge, skill, and experience of caregivers. People who work with young children, regardless of their credentials, are poorly paid, and unfortunately, those who work with infants and toddlers are generally paid least of all.

As our society becomes more aware of the impact of early experiences on later growth and development, we are beginning to pay more attention to who is tending the children. There are now some college and graduate-level programs specifically designed to train teachers to work with this youngest population. If you are lucky, you may find a center that has one of these teachers on staff, either supervising the program or working directly with the infants and toddlers. Generally speaking, however, you are still more likely to see caregivers with little background or training for the work they are doing. Some people who have done baby-sitting or reared children of their own may have terrific instincts. Although they have not had formal training in infant/toddler development, they are intuitively good with young children, genuinely enjoy being around them, and are able to provide the sensitive, stimulating, and loving environment very young children need.

Costs

Infant/toddler centers are extremely expensive to run. This generally means that the cost to parents is high. The major expense for the program usually is, and should be, staffing. If you find a center that does maintain a high staff-child ratio, it may cost as much as $800–900 a month for full-time care, though in some areas good care may be cheaper.

Program Approach

The centers you are likely to see will probably fit more or less into one of three categories: developmentally based care; custodial care; or mini-nursery school. Only the developmentally based approach is really suited to the needs of very young children.

A Developmentally Based Program

All facets of the program—the physical environment, the play materials, the staffing pattern, and the schedule—are based on a good understanding of the developmental needs of babies and toddlers. Group size is small, and the adult-child ratio is high. The teachers in charge have studied infant development and have specifically chosen to work with this age group. There is ongoing training and staff development for assistants and aides. The flow of the day revolves around the needs of each child. Feeding, diapering, napping, and playing are not scheduled group activities. Staffing is consistent, so babies and toddlers can form attachments with particular caregivers, who will be primarily responsible for their physical care. There is a strong emphasis on parent involvement in the program; parents are welcome and encouraged to spend time in the center and at group meetings. Individual conferences are frequent. Such programs are designed to meet the benchmarks of quality described earlier in this chapter.

Why isn't this the solution to everyone's child care needs? It may well be. Unfortunately, these types of programs are few and far between and often very expensive. Because they limit the size of their groups, it is very difficult to get a place in such a program—waiting lists are usually long.

Custodial Care

Some people think all that's involved in the care of very young children is to keep them safe, clean, fed, and diapered. This is sometimes referred to as custodial care. Centers with this approach tend to have large groups of kids and, frequently, an inadequately trained staff. The children are likely to be treated in a fairly regimented fashion. Babies and toddlers are fed, changed, and put to sleep at specific times of the day. They may spend lots of time in playpens or cribs. Although there are toys to play with, the children do not have very much one-to-one time and attention from the caregivers.

This mother describes such a program:

One very large room was divided by partitions into several smaller areas. The only decorations were Disney decals, no artwork done by children. The place was very clean and very bare. In fact, there was a man vacuuming right there in the middle of the morning—it seemed to scare some of the children. Several toddlers were in a room with a very young-looking caregiver. She was changing their diapers one by one on a changing table. The others just sat waiting on the rug. There were no toys in sight. When I asked about playthings, the caregiver pointed to a closed cabinet. All the kids were in diapers and T-shirts. I was told this was routine, so they wouldn't mess up their clothes. It was eerie. I felt like they got fed, diapered, and had naps, but there was very little adult attention or opportunities for play. I wanted to report them to someone but realized they weren't doing anything illegal. It was depressing.

People who run this kind of center may be perfectly well intentioned, but they are not taking into account that babies and toddlers have needs beyond the obvious physical ones. Very young children need a lot of conversation and stimulation. They need to be cuddled and sung to and picked up when they cry. But custodial-care centers are generally trying to handle as many infants and toddlers as possible. This situation simply does not allow for the kind of stimulating and loving environment that is crucial for the healthy development of young children.

Mini-Nursery School

These programs are run by people who mistakenly think that infants and toddlers are just miniature three- and four-year-olds. They design the program on a nursery school model—expecting infants and toddlers to participate in activities that are appropriate for preschool children. You may be told that a center has a "real curriculum" for infants and toddlers, that "real learning" takes place, and that the children's activities yield tangible results, such as paintings, drawings, counting, and learning the ABCs. There are likely to be scheduled times for group stories and music activities, where little ones are expected to hold hands, do circle dances, and sing together.

Such an environment is inappropriate for very young children. They are not ready to be members of a group. Their learning takes place from interacting one-to-one with significant adults and from exploring an environment designed for their physical and mental stage of development. Sometimes such programs have credentialed teachers on their staffs who have worked in elementary schools or nursery schools but have not studied infant and toddler development.

What about Two-Year-Olds?

Two-year-olds can handle a bit more structure than infants and young toddlers—for instance, eating together, napping at a defined time, doing some activities as a group. However, they still need a great deal of individual attention and flexibility from their caregivers. It is fine to offer group activities, but there shouldn't be the expectation that all children will participate. Planning for this age group requires an understanding that attention spans are short and that it is an important part of a two-year-old's development to be able to assert his own identity. This stage is the natural predecessor to being able to enjoy being part of a group.

Finding an Infant/Toddler Center

If you have access to a child care resource and referral agency (page 203), the counselors will be able to tell you if there are infant/toddler centers in your area and give you some information about the specific programs. They will also be able to tell you about any local licensing standards. If there are only a few centers where you live, you may have to apply way in advance of the time you will need care, perhaps even during your pregnancy if you will need care for a young infant. If you will be looking for care for a toddler, the rule of thumb in many cities is to begin your search a year ahead. The directors of the individual programs will tell you when they start taking applications for the following year and whether you can place your name on a waiting list.

If you do not have access to a CCRR group, community-based organizations such as churches, synagogues, YMCAs, nursery schools, and elementary schools may be a good source of information. Ask other parents whether they know of local centers, and as a last resort, look in the phone book for listings of infant/toddler programs.

Contacting Programs

Because your options will probably be limited, it is a good idea to call the director of any program you hear about that may be appropriate for your child. Although you may have received some of this information from your local child care resource and referral organization, it's a good idea to ask these basic questions when you contact the center directly:

- What age children do they care for?
- What hours of care are provided?
- Will they have an opening for someone of your child's age at the time you need care?
- What is the maximum number of children they will accept in a group?
- How many caregivers are with each group of children?
- Are the children divided by age or in a mixed group?
- What are the qualifications of the staff?
- Does the program run year-round?
- What are the fees?
- Is the program licensed?

If the answers to these questions sound good, arrange to visit. It may be helpful to take the following checklist with you.

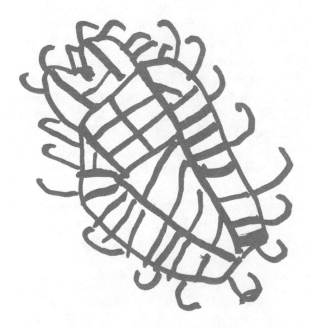

INFANT/TODDLER CENTER CHECKLIST

Name of program _____ Date visited _____

BASIC INFORMATION

___ Hours are suitable

___ Fees are affordable

___ Program is licensed

PHYSICAL SPACE/SAFETY

___ Building safe, clean, well maintained

___ Room light/well ventilated

___ Space designed for active and quiet play

___ Separate area for diapering

___ Separate area for napping

___ Fire alarm/smoke detectors, fire extinguishers/alternate exits

___ Hazardous supplies out of reach

___ Window guards/gates on stairs/covers on radiators/caps on electrical sockets

STAFF

___ Director is accessible and responsive

___ Enough adults to provide individual attention

CAREGIVERS

___ are comfortable with physical aspects of care

___ respond promptly to signs of distress

___ talk directly to infants and toddlers

___ set limits consistently and gently

___ work well with each other

___ allow children to explore/give help when needed

PROGRAM

___ Scheduling is flexible to meet individual needs

___ Appropriate materials are easily accessible

Equipment for babies includes: ___ soft toys ___ rattles ___ mobiles ___ squeeze toys ___ cardboard books

For toddlers, there should also be: ___ push and pull toys ___ riding toys ___ instruments ___ crayons ___ water play

PARENT INVOLVEMENT

___ System for daily communication with staff

___ Scheduled parent/caregiver meetings

___ Parents welcome in the center anytime

COMMENTS

The Visit

In order to get a clear picture of the way the center operates, you should plan to spend at least a half day there. Your visit should give you the chance to observe the room your child would be in, to tour the entire facility—other classrooms, kitchen, outdoor space—and to talk to the director.

Observing

Plan to spend *at least* two hours in the room where your child would be. It is best to get there early in the morning so you can see the interaction between parents, children, and staff as families arrive.

Try to blend into the background so you will see and hear what goes on typically. Of course, the caregivers and children will be aware of your presence on some level, but try not to become part of what is going on —save your questions and comments for a time when you can talk alone with the director.

Notice how families are greeted when they arrive. Are the caregivers ready to receive the children? Do they come right over and say hello to both parent and child? Do the caregivers help a parent get ready to leave by holding the baby or toddler and engaging him in some activity? Do they make sure that parents say goodbye and reassure even the youngest baby with comments like, "Mommy [or Daddy] is going now, but will come back later."

This mother expresses her pleasure at the way her toddler's teacher handles morning goodbyes:

Whenever a parent has to go and the child is sad, Lynn is right there to offer physical and moral support. She holds the child and says, "Mommy (or Daddy) loves you very much but has to go now. She will come back later." She repeats these phrases but allows the child to cry and acknowledges, "I know it makes you sad." Then she gets a book or toy and helps the child get involved. It's so reassuring to walk out of that room when you've got to go.

The Environment

In order to use your time well during your visit to the center, it's important to know what to focus on. First, tune in to your senses and pay attention to your immediate responses to the surroundings. Does the environment appeal to you visually? Is what you see pleasant? Is the room bright and cheerful? Is it clean? Is the temperature comfortable—not too hot or cold? Does the air smell fresh? How many babies or toddlers are in the room? How many adults? Whose voices do you hear? Are the adults speaking softly? Are any children crying? If so, are they receiving comfort?

As you look around the environment, consider the ages of the children and the daily activities that will be going on. The space should be well equipped for, and designed around, those activities.

First, let's consider the basics. Young children spend a lot of time eating, sleeping, and being changed. Check on the following:

Feeding

Where are the babies fed? Are there comfortable chairs where adults can hold and feed infants? For older babies or toddlers, are there high chairs? Are they in good condition? Do they have safety belts? Where is the food stored? Are the bottles kept clean and individually labeled? If there are two-year-olds, do they eat together at a table? Are the chairs sturdy and the right size?

Sleeping

Where do the children sleep? Is there a separate area that can be made quiet and dark? Can the children be seen and heard by the caregivers when they are sleeping? Are the cribs safe and clean? Cribs take up a lot of space, so sometimes more than one child will be using the same crib at different times. If this is the case, each child should have his own sheets and covers in the crib when it is his time for sleeping. Are the mattresses in good condition? Are there bumper guards? Are there mobiles for young babies to watch and listen to as they go to sleep? If there are two-year-olds in the group, do they have cots? Are the cots sturdy and clean?

Diapering

Is the changing area clean and well equipped? Are diapers, wipes, and ointments all within the caregiver's reach? Is there a safety belt on the changing table? Is clean paper laid down for each baby and discarded immediately after use? Is there a diaper pail with a lid that closes firmly? Is there a sink right near the changing area? Do caregivers wash after every diaper change? If there are toddlers or two-year-olds in the group, are there potties available? Are they cleaned immediately after use?

What Other Activities Should the Room Accommodate?

The space should be designed to encourage the babies or toddlers to explore the environment freely and safely. Check on the following:

Layout of the room

Does the space seem adequate for the number of children and adults who are using it? Is there enough open space for crawling and toddling? Is the surface of the floor safe and clean? At least part of the room should be carpeted, so babies and toddlers can move about safely.

In addition to open areas, there should be cozy spaces, partitioned by shelves or other equipment. Very young children need time to get away from the group, explore a toy by themselves, or play one-to-one with a caregiver. The room should be designed in such a way that the adults can see the children wherever they are and get to them easily and quickly.

Are there couches, chairs, or large pillows for children to crawl on and cuddle with caregivers? Where and how are toys kept? Are they visible and accessible to the children? They should be placed on the floor or on low shelves. Very young children cannot ask for toys that are stored away in boxes or closets. The general atmosphere should be inviting for young children and have a comfortable, homelike feeling, as this parent so aptly describes:

What I get upset about is that some of the centers look so sterile and clean. I would like more of a homey atmosphere, where the teacher has put together a little area where the children can go off and be by themselves. There should be a lot of selection of what the kids can play with right where they can reach rather than putting everything on the shelf with nothing on the floor and pictures hung up too high for the children to see. People should know that a sterile, clean environment means hands-off. Children's work environment is their toys —spread out.

Toys

Toys should be washable, safe for young children to put in their mouths, and range from simple to more complex. They should be the right size for little hands to manipulate, with no small parts that can be broken off and swallowed. There should be variety in the kinds of play things available and enough of them for the size of the group.

Look for the kind of toys that respond to a child's action—for instance, rattles that make noise when shaken; balls that can be rolled or tossed; nesting toys; large plastic beads that can be snapped together and pulled apart; cuddly stuffed animals and dolls. For toddlers, look for toys that can be pulled and pushed, stacked, taken apart and put together. For two-year-olds, there should also be simple puzzles, cardboard building blocks, cars and trucks. Books should have cloth or cardboard pages and simple, clear, colorful pictures.

If the space is large enough, there should be a small slide, a rocking boat, a bouncing horse, or some other piece of equipment where children can exercise their large muscles.

Is there a record player or tape recorder? A piano? Are there different kinds of music to listen to? Are there instruments to play? Even very young babies enjoy listening to music, and toddlers and twos delight in making music, singing, and dancing.

Walls

The walls should be clean and decorated with simple, colorful pictures of people, animals, and other familiar objects. These should be placed at the children's eye level. It is reassuring to very young children to have pictures of their families on display, so they can "check in" when they are feeling lonely. Do you see such pictures? There should be a mirror where the children can see themselves. Each child should have a cubby or space on a shelf for personal belongings.

You will have to rely on the *feeling* the environment gives you. Does it seem clean and comfortable for adults and young children? Is there variety in color and texture? Consider the following positive and negative words in rating the environment:

It should be *inviting;* it should *not* be *overwhelming.* It should feel *friendly* and *cozy.* It should *not* feel *cluttered* or *confining.*

This Boston mother was delighted to find just such a place:

I never thought I would consider center care until I came here. It is the most warm, nurturing, comforting, cozy space that I've ever been in. The teachers are so giving to the babies and to us. Whenever I go there, I feel like I don't ever want to leave.

Observe the Staff

The most important aspect of an infant or toddler's environment is the adults who care for him. Watch and listen carefully to how the caregivers interact with the children and each other.

With infants, you should see caregivers who:

- provide lots of physical contact—holding, carrying, rocking on laps.
- engage in one-to-one interaction with babies, talking and making frequent eye contact.
- respond to the various sounds that babies make, imitating and encouraging their vocalizations.
- use simple and repetitive language to point out things in the environment and narrate activities that the baby is engaged in.
- react quickly and lovingly to babies who are crying or showing other signs of distress.
- feed individual babies when they are hungry.
- diaper babies whenever necessary.
- allow babies to nap when they are tired.
- handle babies gently and lovingly when feeding or changing them.

- encourage babies' attempts at independence—reaching for toys, crawling, trying to stand. Tell the baby how wonderful she is, with genuine enthusiasm: "Yes, Susie, you got that toy! Yes you did. What a strong baby you are!"
- communicate easily and in a calm voice with the other caregivers in the room, ensuring a well-organized flow of activity. If, for instance, one caregiver is occupied changing a baby, others should be attentively supervising those at play.
- carefully follow health procedures—washing hands after every diaper change and before feedings. Keep bottles clean and identified for each baby. Store food in the refrigerator—jars of baby food should be labeled for each child and dated. All eating utensils should be thoroughly washed with hot water and soap.
- take babies outside for some time each day unless the weather is too cold or it is raining or snowing.
- make sure each infant has opportunities to experience different aspects of the environment—some time on the floor, in an infant seat, carried over the shoulder.

Notice whether individual adults in the room seem to have special relationships with particular babies. Although children at a center often have to interact with several adults, it is best for each baby to have a consistent relationship with one caregiver, who usually feeds, changes, and puts him to sleep. This makes it possible for the particular caregiver to really get to know the child and be able to recognize when he is tired, hungry, overwhelmed, or in the mood for play. It allows the child to focus on one important adult rather than having to adapt to differing styles of care—a tiring task for a very young baby.

You should NOT see:

- infants spending long periods of time confined in playpens, infant seats, or cribs when they are obviously bored or uncomfortable.
- caregivers involved in long discussions with each other and not attending to the babies.
- any rough physical handling of young babies.
- loud or harsh talking.
- crying babies left unattended.
- all babies fed, changed, or put to sleep at the same time.
- babies fed in cribs with their bottles propped up. Babies too young to hold their own bottles should *always* be fed in the arms of a caregiver.
- fewer caregivers present than is appropriate (see previously stated guidelines). If a caregiver is on a break or is out sick, another, preferably familiar, adult should substitute.
- babies abruptly moved about without explanation from the caregiver as to what is happening next.

With toddlers and two-year-olds, you should see caregivers who:

- encourage language development by naming objects, describing events in simple terms, and helping children express themselves by expanding on what they say. For example, when a toddler says, "Jimmy ball," the caregiver might respond, "Yes, Jimmy is rolling the ball."
- understand and comply with young children's need for repetition by patiently reading the same story, singing the same song, playing the same game several times when requested.
- recognize that testing limits and saying no is a normal part of a toddler's development, the way he begins to establish his own sense of self. Caregivers should respond to this behavior calmly, with as much flexibility as possible. If a limit must be set for safety reasons, this

should be explained simply, while the caregiver offers the toddler a way out that will maintain his self-respect. "Banging on the window could hurt you, because the glass can break. Here's a good pot you can bang on."

- respect a young child's growing desire to be independent by offering simple choices: "Would you like this big ball or this little one?"; "Do you want an apple or banana for snack today?"
- encourage the child when she tries to do something for herself. "You want to put on your own sock? Good, let me just help you get started."
- offer help when a toddler is becoming frustrated with an activity that is too difficult, or guide him to something he can do by himself.
- give lots of praise for accomplishments.
- recognize that children of this age are not yet able to share; provide more than one of the most popular toys; offer substitutes when a child can't have what she wants when she wants it, promising she will have a turn, and then making sure she gets it.
- actively participate in the games toddlers initiate; drinking from the cup that is offered and commenting on the "delicious tea"; holding the baby doll and rocking it to sleep.
- frequently read to the children one-to-one or in small groups.
- provide a variety of materials to experiment with—large crayons, play dough, finger paints, sand, water.
- feed toddlers when they are hungry. If the children are fed in a group, there should be enough adults so that no child has to wait too long and so those who need help get it promptly.
- encourage attempts at self-feeding by giving children finger foods; child-size utensils; cups, with lids, that right themselves when tipped.
- make sure toddlers spend time outdoors each day, with a chance to get vigorous exercise on riding toys, slides, and swings.
- let children rest when they are tired and sleep when they need to.

You should NOT see:

- anybody insisting that the children participate in an activity, unless it is for safety reasons—i.e., a fire drill, or a time when everyone is going outside and there is no adult available to stay behind with one child.
- adults who react angrily when toddlers or twos say no to a direction or request.
- children fighting over toys, without adult intervention.

- caregivers making fun of the way a young child speaks or responding to his language with baby talk.
- use of any type of physical punishment or rough handling of children.
- caregivers reacting with disgust or annoyance when children need to be changed or get dirty.
- toddlers made to use potties before they are ready; caregivers who humiliate them for being in diapers, telling them they are babies, or comparing them to other children who are already trained.
- children forced to sit on potties for long periods of time, until they "produce," or scolded for soiling their clothes.
- toddlers sitting in high chairs or at the table for long periods before food is ready.
- food used as a bribe, reward, or punishment.
- toddlers scolded for being messy when they eat.
- children eating foods that can cause choking, such as: uncooked carrots, celery, hot dogs (unless they are skinless), grapes (unless they are peeled), nuts, popcorn. Honey has been found to cause respiratory failure in some infants and toddlers, and it should not be used as a sweetener for children under the age of two. If you see these foods, tell the staff that they are hazardous. Few people who have not taken health and safety courses have this information.
- children denied access to a security blanket, stuffed animal, or other treasure.

Getting the Full Picture

After you have spent time observing the room your child would be in, make sure to check other classrooms as well. After all, if you have a baby now, she will soon be a toddler, so it's important to know what the toddler room is like.

Take a walk around the entire facility so you can check on the overall safety and suitability of the environment. Is the building in good shape? No paint peeling from the walls, no hazardous exposed electrical wiring? If the program is located on the ground floor, check that there are at least two exits in case of fire. If it's located on an upper floor, make sure to find out the center's evacuation plan in the event of fire or other emergencies.

Are there fire extinguishers? Smoke detectors? Are there periodic fire drills? Are radiators and electrical outlets covered? Are there win-

dow guards? Are all hazardous substances secured out of reach of the children?

If there is a kitchen, is it clean? Is it well equipped? Is the food fresh? Is the kitchen area inaccessible to young children without the supervision of an adult?

If there is an outdoor play area, is the surface safe for young children —rubber matting, sand, grass? There should be play equipment, such as slides, swings, jungle gyms, tricycles, that are the right scale for little people. Are they in good condition? If there is a sandbox, is the sand clean? Is it covered at night? Is the play yard enclosed so no child can wander off without an adult?

If the program does not have its own outdoor play space, find out where the children are taken. How far away is the play area? Do toddlers walk there? Are children wheeled in strollers, pulled in a little cart, carried in back packs? Are there enough staff members present to make the trip safely? Make sure to go to look at the playground or park, and use these criteria to check on its safety features.

Talk with the Director

The director usually sets the policy and tone of the program as well as hiring and supervising the staff. It's important that you like this person and feel comfortable talking openly about your concerns. Go over what you observed at the center; bring up anything you didn't understand or found troubling. Ask about the times of the day you didn't see. For instance, if you didn't see any children napping, ask what happens when a child seems tired and whether there are scheduled nap times. If the group didn't go outside while you were there, ask if it does and how often and where.

Make sure to ask the following questions:

- Is the program licensed?
- How long has the center been running?
- How much staff turnover is there? Ask specific questions: Will the caregiver you observed actually be the one with your baby? How long have the individual caregivers been with the center?
- What qualifications does she look for in hiring staff?
- What is the maximum number of children in each group?

- What is the minimum staff-child ratio at any point in the day? Put it more specifically: How many children will be in your child's group? How many caregivers will regularly be present? What's the minimum number of adults who will be on duty at any point in the day?

- What is the center's policy about illness? Under what circumstances would you be expected to keep your child home or come to pick her up if she seems ill? This is an important issue, because disease spreads quickly in groups of young children. Guidelines should include: not having a child in the center if there is fever, vomiting, severe diarrhea, unexplained rash, signs of conjunctivitis (pink-eye). If your child develops any of these symptoms while in the center, you should expect to be called and to pick her up promptly. In the event of any accident or injury more serious than a minor scrape or bruise, you should be notified.

- If the center provides meals, find out what kind of foods are served. Is there a good balance of protein, vegetables, fruits? Are sweets served? If so, how often? Ask if you will be able to see weekly menus.

- Does anyone on the staff have training in first aid? Is there a well-equipped first-aid kit? What physician or hospital emergency room does the center use if immediate action is required?

- What are the payment policies? Are you expected to pay weekly, monthly, yearly? Are there additional fees for diapers, milk, etc.? Are you expected to supply such items? Which ones, specifically?

- What is the calendar for the year? It is important for you to know in advance what days the center will be closed, since you may have to make alternative arrangements to cover those times.

A well-organized program should provide you with health and emergency forms. You should make sure the center has accurate, up-to-date information on your work addresses, phone numbers, the name of your pediatrician, and whom you would want the center to call in an emergency if you can't be reached.

You should give the names of the specific people who have permission to pick up your child. The center should assure you that your child won't be released to anyone else without your prior permission.

Ask about Parental Involvement

How do parents and caregivers arrange to communicate? Will you have time to talk with the caregivers in the morning and at pickup time? Is there a system for leaving notes? A chart about what your baby or toddler ate that day, how and when she slept, etc.?

This mother looks forward to the daily notes she receives about her toddler:

It's wonderful. Every day, the teachers leave personal notes about what Max did and how the day went. They really pay attention, and share things that they know are important to us. One day, his teacher left us a note saying that Max had approached her and managed to tell her that he needed some love. She gave him a big hug, and told us that it made her day! Another time, after he had been absent for a few days, she left us a note about how glad the other kids were to have him back, the things they said, the affection they showed him. We love the notes and are saving all of them.

Ask if you are welcome to spend time in the center whenever you can. If you work nearby, can you come in at a certain time of day to visit your baby? Are there regularly scheduled parent meetings and conferences? Can you help out if you have a free morning or afternoon? *Never leave your child in any program that tells you it has a policy that does not allow parents to be present at certain times. You should always be able to have access to your child.*

Bottles; Pacifiers; Toilet Training

Ask whether the center has a set policy about the age when a baby or toddler should stop using a bottle. Is the use of pacifiers restricted? Is toilet training begun at a specific age?

Be wary if the answer to any of these questions is yes. These are important milestones in the lives of young children, but each child has her own road map and timetable. There is no one "correct" time to stop the bottle, eliminate the pacifier, or begin toilet training. These major steps depend on the individual baby or toddler's stage of readiness.

A more appropriate approach is for the center's staff to discuss these issues with you as they arise. Make sure that no changes will be made in your baby's usual routine without your approval. You are the one who should decide the time for switching to solid foods, weaning from a bottle or pacifier, and beginning toilet training.

Talk about Your Own Child's Needs

Ask any specific question you have about your child's care. For instance, if you have been nursing and want to provide bottled breast milk for your baby instead of formula, will that be acceptable? Ask if the caregivers have had experience with babies who are making the transition from breast to bottle. How do they recommend you go about helping your baby make the change?

Perhaps while you were observing you noticed that some of the children your child's age are already out of diapers, but you are sure your toddler is not yet ready. Will the staff be comfortable sticking with diapers until you both agree he is ready to try the potty? What kinds of signs do they look for to indicate that readiness?

Your toddler seems very attached to the pacifier and you are not sure how long to let it continue. What do they think? Will it bother them if he uses it a lot during the day?

By asking these kinds of detailed questions, you can find out how much experience the people at the center have, how sensitive they are to working with individual children and parents, and what their philosophy of child rearing is. The best approach will involve ongoing communication, where you and the caregivers together will figure out what is best for your baby or toddler in any situation. Make sure you feel comfortable. You are considering leaving a very young child in someone else's care. You have the right to know exactly how that care will be carried out.

One child care worker in a center for infants and toddlers talks about what she observed:

I tell parents, "You have to do it for your child and for yourself, because you are not going to feel happy to go to work if there is something that really bothers you about the center. It is good for you to get strength and know that you can ask anything you want to and they are supposed to answer any questions you have."

Making Your Decision

Think about what you have observed and been told. If you had negative feelings about the environment, the caregivers, or the director, trust your instincts and look elsewhere. If you felt positive but still need more information, ask to visit again or send your spouse for a visit. A center director should welcome your questions and try to give you the information and time you need to make a decision. The center may need to know your decision within a certain time if other parents are waiting, but don't feel pushed into making a commitment if you still have doubts. Even though in many parts of the country it's hard to find a good center for this age group, this is a situation where something is not necessarily better than nothing. If you don't feel that the centers you've seen are right for your family, consider another child care option.

You may have to make some accommodations. Perhaps the space is not quite as big as you think it should be or the center will be closed more often than you would like. You should not, however, compromise on the quality of care your child will receive. Do you like the philosophy of the program and the way the caregivers relate to children and parents? Are the sizes of the groups appropriate for the ages of the children? Is the adult-child ratio good? These are the most important issues to consider.

Getting Started

When you have found a program you like, make sure to let the director know as soon as possible, so you won't lose your space. Before leaving your child in the center's care, make sure you have provided all the necessary health and emergency information.

The program should have a plan for how to phase young children in. The method should be based on the staff's experience and an understanding of how to best help very young children and parents deal with separation. However, if you have a different idea of what your baby or toddler needs, you should certainly speak up and discuss modifying the usual procedure.

This New York mother did exactly that:

I was sending my twenty-two-month-old daughter to a day care center. She had spent some time at our house with a baby-sitter, but this was going to be her first time away from home. The center told me to stay for the first day and plan to leave her there alone for some time on the second day. Julia is a pretty secure kid, but even so, just one morning with me there didn't seem enough. I said that I wanted to hang around for a few days and leave for short periods when I felt she was ready. Then, when she was really comfortable, I would leave for the whole day. The teacher didn't seem too pleased with my plan, but she went along with it and it worked out very well. After three days, I spent just a half hour settling her in, and left for work. Julia said a cheerful goodbye to me and had a good time the rest of the day. When I said goodbye the next few mornings I noticed several other children crying, and I couldn't help thinking they were left before they were ready. A few years later, when I brought my son to the same program, they had changed their policy drastically. Now, parents were expected to be available for the first two weeks to phase their kids in gradually.

At different ages and stages, babies and toddlers are more or less adaptable to new surroundings and people. Very young infants, under the age of six months, may adapt more quickly to a loving and friendly caregiver than a baby of seven, eight, or nine months who really knows her parents' style, and may feel fearful in a new situation. Toddlers at certain stages may alternately feel eager to be independent and scared to be. For such young children, it would not make sense to discuss your plans too far in advance. If you have a toddler or two-year-old, simply mention the day before that you will be going somewhere to play with other children. Do not tell your child that you will ultimately be leaving her there without you. Such information would certainly make her anxious. By the time you are ready to leave her, she will know the caregivers, be familiar with the environment and be better prepared to handle the separation.

The two children in the following family reacted quite differently:

My son was ten months when he first went to a center. It went smoothly because I used to take him with me to that same place from the time he was an infant whenever I picked his sister up. He was familiar with the setting, so by the time he started, there was no transition problem. He went right in and did just fine. I stayed around a few minutes and that's all. With his sister, I took her for an hour one day and two hours the next day and three hours the next, until she got used to it.

Whatever the age of your child or the center's policy, you should definitely plan to be available for at least a few days to help your child get acclimated to the surroundings and the caregivers. How many days this process will take will depend on your child's age, stage, and personal reaction to separation from you. If you cannot take more than a few days off from your job and feel your child still needs support, arrange to have another familiar and loved adult—grandma, good friend, baby-sitter—stay with your child. Work out your plan with the staff so you can all support your baby or toddler in making a smooth adjustment. You will probably need this time as well. It isn't easy to leave a very young child in a new situation. When you do, it's important that you feel confident that your child is in good hands. Your baby or toddler will be sensitive to your emotional attitude, so try to make mornings as relaxed as you can.

This can be very difficult when you have to go through the kind of routine this Southern mother describes:

You always need about three arms to carry everything: bag for the baby, the diapers, the formula, then you still forget something—the pacifiers, for example. Then of course you have to get up two or three hours earlier than you normally would, to get the baby ready and then get yourself ready and make sure everybody is cool and collected as you walk out the door. I've worked a full day before I get to work.

It may help to do as much as you can each night before you go to bed. Have the baby bag packed, the stroller by the door, extra clothes set out in case the baby soils the first set you put on. If you keep extra diapers, bottles, pacifiers, and clothes at the center, you won't have to worry so much about forgetting things as you walk out the door.

When you are ready to leave your child, you can help make things easier by:

- making sure your baby or toddler has made contact with one of the caregivers who can provide support when you leave.
- saying goodbye clearly to both the caregiver and your child. Even with a very young child, it's important that you say you are going and when you will be back. Toddlers can't tell time, so give your child a reference that is concrete and will have meaning to her: "I will come back after you have your banana" or ". . . when Sally says it's time for mommies and daddies to be coming now." *Never sneak away without saying goodbye, even if your child is happily occupied. Working*

through saying goodbye is an important part of the child care experience for you, your child, and the caregiver.

■ making sure your baby or toddler has everything she needs—her bottle, pacifier, special blanket or stuffed animal, sheets and covers.

■ checking with the caregiver as to what would be a good time to call in and find out how things are going.

■ making sure to come back at the time you said you would.

The Ongoing Relationship

Caring for very young children is a demanding job for both parents and caregivers. Each needs the support of the other. There are several ways you can contribute to making your relationship run smoothly:

■ Be sure to come at the agreed upon times in the morning and evening.

■ Check regularly on your child's supply of diapers, food, and other necessities, so caregivers won't have to spend time searching or borrowing from others.

■ Leave time in your schedule to settle your child in each morning and help him separate from the center at the end of the day. Rushing through arrival and departure rituals can be unsettling for you both.

■ Keep the caregivers informed about how your child is eating and sleeping. Let them know if any particular events may be affecting your child's behavior—a family crisis, a sick pet, a visiting relative.

■ If *anything* concerns you about the care your child is receiving, bring it up promptly. It isn't easy to have a good discussion when you are delivering or picking up your child, so ask the caregiver when you might talk on the phone or set up a meeting.

■ Attend parent meetings.

■ Spend time in the center helping out if you have a free morning or afternoon.

■ Let the caregivers know that you appreciate the good care they are providing for your child.

If you have made a careful selection and follow these guidelines, chances are things will go smoothly. But even in the best situations, there may be times when your very young child does not want to go to the center. This may have nothing to do with the care he is receiving, but may merely reflect a stage in his own development. For example: When you started your baby at five months old, he may have been complacent and content. Now, at a year old, he may suddenly shriek when you get ready to go. If such problems arise, talk them through with the caregivers. Odds are, you can work them out by making some minor changes—stay a little longer in the mornings for a few days or give your child something special from home to keep at the center.

If, however, your child is consistently unhappy and you cannot solve the problem with the caregivers, you may need to consider making a change. In Chapter 11, "Changing Child Care Arrangements," we will discuss how to handle that situation.

Early Childhood Centers

*E*arly childhood centers provide education and care for groups of young children. These programs may be called preschools, day care centers, nursery schools, or early childhood development centers. Until recently, nursery schools were the most common of these programs. They provided a social and educational experience, primarily for three- and four-year-olds, through part-time programs. They were not designed to meet the needs of working parents, though many of them have now responded to the changing times by offering full-day programs.

Day care centers exist specifically to provide education and care for the children of parents who work full-time. Typical hours are from 6:00 A.M. to 6:00 P.M. in some parts of the country and from 8:00 A.M. to 6:00 P.M. in others. Good day care centers provide the same kind of educational and social experiences that we associate with nursery schools.

Head Start, a government-sponsored preschool program, gives three-

and four-year-old children from low-income families the opportunity for an enriched preschool experience. Head Start has not been geared to working parents. Programs generally offer either a morning or afternoon option.

In some areas of the country, public school systems are now offering prekindergarten programs that may provide another option for parents of four-year-olds. Unfortunately, most of these programs also run for only three hours a day; only a few are open for a full school day.

Who Operates Early Childhood Centers?

Many nursery schools and day care centers are run as nonprofit corporations, sponsored by community organizations, such as churches, synagogues, or YMCA's. Some are parent cooperatives. More and more early childhood programs are operated as profit-making businesses. These may be small mom-and-pop-style operations or centers run either by local companies or by large corporations that license franchises around the country.

When Are the Centers Open?

Many centers committed to serving working parents are open year-round. Some, however, follow a ten- or eleven-month calendar, closing for all or part of the summer and for extended vacations during the winter and spring holidays. The schedules vary from place to place and from center to center.

What Hours of Care Are Provided?

A variety of time options may be offered: mornings or afternoons; school hours—for example, 8:30 to 4:00; or full-time care. Where full-time care begins at 8:00 in the morning and ends at 6:00 in the evening, the assumption is that parents who work from 9:00 to 5:00 can meet this schedule. This is frequently not the case, however, as this mother describes:

I work quite a distance from where my children are and have to pick them both up by six o'clock, at each kid's center. It creates a lot of stress because it's so unpredictable. First of all, it's very difficult to leave my job at exactly 5:00 P.M. which I have to do in order not to get into terrible traffic. What happens is, it's more like leaving at 5:15 P.M., driving frantically, trying every route possible, and still being late periodically.

Do Parents Participate in the Center's Operation?

Parents may be encouraged to serve on a center's board of directors and play an active role in defining policy, balancing the budget, and recruiting for the program, or they may simply be asked to participate in fundraising and social events. In some centers, there is not much involvement at all, nor is it really encouraged. In parent cooperatives, parents generally hire the director and teaching staff, make major decisions about the program and the facility, organize and run fund-raising projects, handle recruitment and admissions, and may also spend time working in the classrooms.

Government Regulation

Most states now have procedures for licensing early childhood programs. Regulations deal with such issues as the safety and size of the physical plant; limitations on group size; adult-child ratios; and teacher qualifications. However, these requirements vary tremendously. In New York City, for instance, directors of early childhood programs are required to have a master's degree in early childhood education and at least two years of teaching experience. Group teachers are required to have at least a bachelor's degree in early childhood education. For children three to four years of age, total group size is limited to fifteen. For children from four to five years of age, total group size is limited to twenty. Unfortunately, such regulations are far from typical. Many states do not require *any prior education or training* for teachers and set no limits on group size.

What does this mean for your family? Obviously, it's better to have regulation than not, but even if your state has fairly good licensing requirements, this does not necessarily mean that every center will provide good care. And in the states where there are minimal or no requirements, many programs still aspire to meeting high standards.

Ultimately, *you* really have to know what makes for a quality program, regardless of the local requirements.

What Are the Keys to Quality?

Three factors are extremely important in providing a quality setting for preschool children: 1) the size of the group should not be too large; 2) there should be enough adults present to manage the group safely and give individual attention to the children (the adult-child ratio); 3) the teachers should have a good understanding of the physical, social, and educational needs of the age group.

The National Association for the Education of Young Children (NAEYC), an organization of teachers and others concerned with the growth and development of young children, has recommended the following minimum standards for early childhood centers:

- A *maximum* group size of twenty children for three-, four-, or five-year-olds, with *at least two teachers*—an adult-child ratio of 1:10.
- Program directors should have *at least* a bachelor's degree in early childhood education or child development.
- Group teachers should have *as a minimum* a degree in early childhood education from a two-year program.
- All teaching staff, including assistant teachers and teacher aides, should be involved in ongoing in-service training to upgrade their skills.

Finding an Early Childhood Center

If there is a child care resource and referral agency in your area (see page 203), the counselors will talk with you about your options and refer you to programs near where you live or work. They will have information about the cost of center care in your community and other details about specific programs. If there are licensing standards for early childhood center programs in your area, the CCRR will only refer you to centers that meet legal requirements.

If you do not have access to such a group, the best way to locate early childhood programs is to ask other parents and to contact community organizations—YMCAs, churches, synagogues, and your local public school. If you are still having difficulty, check listings for nursery schools and day care centers in the yellow pages.

Contacting Center Programs

Generally speaking, you need to begin your search almost a year before the time you will want your child to enter a program. Some programs begin taking applications as early as November or December for placement the following September. Many accept children on a first-come, first-served basis, but some programs have more complicated admission procedures. They may want to interview you; some may want to interview your child. Consider the impact such a process could have on your child. The particular criteria that programs use in evaluating whom they select may or may not be clear, but even very young children may be aware when they are being "tested," and rejection may hurt. You can make things easier by explaining to your child beforehand that she will be playing with some toys and talking to someone at the center so she can see how she likes it.

When you call a center, ask whether they expect to have openings at the time you will need a place for your child. Then find out whether the program:

- is licensed.
- offers the hours of care you need.
- is affordable.

Ask also:

- What is the maximum number of children in a group?
- How many teachers are with each group?
- What are the qualifications of the teachers?
- Does the program have a particular educational philosophy?

Some programs follow a very specific educational model. For instance, you might be told that the center is a Montessori school, uses the open-classroom approach, or the Waldorf method, either adhering to the philosophy pretty closely or else loosely following its tenets. You may not have time to read what each of these approaches means. It is, however, important to ask the director to explain the approach carefully and to give you any written statements the school may have about its philosophy of education.

If the information you gather leaves you with a positive impression, schedule a time when you can visit the center.

The Visit

Since you will probably want to visit more than one program, it is best not to bring your child along, as this Midwest mother explains:

I didn't take my daughter with me when I was just looking around. Maybe I'm wrong, but I think, until you narrow it down, you should not take your child with you because it gets confusing for them. My daughter would be concerned in thinking about all the different places.

Plan to go as an observer, and take with you the checklist that appears at the end of this chapter. If you are only visiting one or two programs, you will probably get the most out of your visit by spending a half day, with a couple of hours in the classroom. If you have a number of centers to see, you may not be able to take this much time away from work. Try to get to the center early in the morning and plan to spend two or three hours, including *at least* an hour observing the classroom your child would be in. Then look at the entire facility, and talk in detail with the director.

When you enter the classroom, pay attention to your immediate impressions. What your eyes see, what your ears hear, what you feel about the room is probably very similar to what your child will experience. Scan the room. Do you see a variety of colors and textures? Is the room bright and well ventilated? Do you see children's artwork displayed on the walls? Is the furniture—tables, chairs, shelves—an appropriate size for young children? Are there cubbies for the children's individual belongings?

Do the children seem to be having fun? Are they involved in activities? In a good program, there is usually a busy sort of hum in the room, pleasant to the ears. You should not hear teachers shouting or speaking harshly or see children who look bored or unhappy.

Look at the Materials and Classroom Setup

The way the room is arranged will tell you a lot about the program and the teachers. The space should be designed to accommodate the variety of activities important in the life of a preschool child. There should be defined areas for different types of activities, as well as some open space where children can come together as a group for stories, meetings, and music.

The actual quality of materials and equipment may vary greatly from center to center. The place may have a flashy look, with new furniture and brand-new toys, or the furniture may be secondhand and some of the materials may have been made by parents or teachers. Fancy and new does not necessarily mean the program is better, though equipment should be clean and in good repair. What matters most is:

- the variety and safety of available materials.
- their accessibility to children.
- the teacher's role in encouraging their use.

How Young Children Learn

In the past few years there has been increasing pressure on parents to begin formal, structured education earlier and earlier. This "superbaby" phenomenon seeks to produce early readers, get young children started on computers—in short, have early childhood programs take on the role of the elementary schools. Since parents want what's best for their children, it is easy to get confused. No parent wants to hold a child back or not prepare him adequately for the skills he will need to master. However, learning is a continuum, and three- and four-year-olds are at a particular stage in this process. Preschool children learn through their interactions with materials and people. They learn by *playing*—seeing, touching, and manipulating things in very concrete ways. Learning to count by rote has little meaning for children of this age. They need to hold three objects to understand the idea of three, and count how many children are at the table to know how many pieces of apple are needed for snack. Although they enjoy reciting the ABCs, for most three-year-olds this is merely a chant, with LMNOP as a favorite letter. Letters and words begin to take on real meaning when children are helped to identify the letters that make their names, have lots of stories read to them, and "write" their own stories, with teachers putting down the words they say and reading them aloud.

These are the kinds of preschool experiences that lay the foundation for the more formal abstract learning experiences in reading and math that will come later. When people refer to the reading- and math-readiness activities that should go on in the preschool classroom, this is what they mean. A well-organized preschool classroom should definitely include the following areas and activities:

Arts and Crafts Area

Paints, crayons, markers, glue, paper, and scissors should be on low shelves easily accessible to the children. There should be easels for painting and a table for other art activities.

In good early childhood programs, certain art activities are planned by the teacher to give children specific experiences and help them develop their skills. For instance, you might see a group of children leafing through magazines, searching for the letters in their names, cutting them out, and pasting them on paper. Or all the children in the art area may be working with only specific colors in different media—blue and red paint, crayons, and paper. Projects like these are appropriate and enjoyable for children of this age.

There should, however, be many opportunities for children to create their own art—to select the materials they like and pursue individual projects. This gives young children great pleasure as well as a sense of mastery when a project is completed. Painting, drawing, gluing, and cutting also help children develop the coordination they will later need for writing. Recognizing colors, contrasts, and shapes lays the foundation for recognizing letters and words.

Block Area

There should be an area of the room set aside for block building, with enough space to make fairly elaborate constructions. You should see wooden blocks, cardboard blocks, and props like toy cars, trucks, people, street signs, and toy animals. Young children delight in constructing buildings, towers, bridges—entire cities. They like to build tall towers and knock them down. Working with blocks gives kids a chance to re-create pieces of the world around them—making a zoo, a farm, the office building where Mommy works. While they build, they learn to recognize different sizes and shapes and how to measure and fit things together. These very concrete experiences give young children the basic foundation they need for later abstract work in mathematics.

Manipulative Toys

You should see a variety of games that involve putting things together, sorting, and matching shapes, colors, and sizes. There should be puzzles, peg boards, small blocks that snap or stick together, Tinkertoy pieces, Lego bricks, Bristle Blocks. Some of these toys work in only one way; puzzles and peg boards, for instance, require a child to find the right match. Tinkertoy pieces and Lego bricks, on the other hand give her a chance to make her own constructions, with no one correct solution except to complete the idea she has in mind. All of these materials challenge young children to organize several parts into something whole, a skill they will need when learning to read, write, and work in math.

Nonstructured Materials

It's important for young children to play with materials they can mold and change. They should have opportunities to use water, sand, clay, and play dough. Water play is a great delight for young children and seems to be very relaxing, as you've probably observed at bath time. Play dough and clay are easy to control, and young children get great pleasure from making long snakes, which can turn into cookies or pizzas with a squish here and a pat there. Sand is fun to sift and pour, make into mountains, and flatten at whim. Such activities help young children to release tension, experiment with the physical properties of these materials, and have fun.

House Area

Some part of the room should be set up as if it were part of a house. You should see clothes for dress-up, hats, household items such as a telephone, pots and pans, a play stove or sink, dolls and doll beds. Preschoolers need the chance to try various roles, explore their fantasies, re-create their own family dramas. This dramatic play allows young children to use their imagination and more fully digest what they are hearing in books and seeing in the world around them. For instance, a child with a new sibling may play out his feelings with a doll. Or a story about fire fighters may come to life as children pretend they are fire fighters in a firehouse, respond to an alarm, and heroically put out the fire.

Book Area

Books, lots of them, should be accessible to children on low shelves, near a comfortable area to read—large pillows, a couch, a soft chair. There should be different kinds of books—some with simple pictures and words, others with more complex stories. There should be books that relate to real-life situations, books about city and country life, animals, trucks, railroads. The selection should include different types of family structures (single-parent families, children with divorced parents, those living with grandparents, aunts and uncles, etc.) Books should include people from different ethnic backgrounds, and stories should not further ethnic or sexual stereotypes. There should also be stories of fantasy so that children can share the adventures of make-believe characters.

Exploring the world of books helps young children reinforce their own experiences and also learn about the world outside their immediate environment. It offers them a way to discuss their own concerns, wishes, and fantasies. Preschoolers enjoy being read to in a group, especially if they are encouraged to answer questions about the story or imitate its actions or sounds. And when one child cuddles up with an adult and shares a book, a strong bond can form between them and reading can seem like great fun. Little kids love to learn poems and rhymes and then to make up their own. They like to "read" books they have heard often, sometimes having memorized them completely. They also like to make books to share with their friends and families. A good preschool program should include all these experiences.

Music and Dance

Children enjoy listening to music and creating their own. They like to form bands and march around in parades. They love to sing and particularly enjoy songs that are accompanied with hand gestures, like "Where Is Thumbkin?" and "The Eensy-Weensy Spider." It is a great asset if a program has a teacher who can play the guitar or piano and lead group sings. There should at least be a record or tape player and records or tapes with music of different types.

There should be a variety of instruments that make different sounds —bells, tambourines, maracas, cymbals. Instruments can also be home-made—cans filled with seeds that make sounds when shaken; drums made of coffee tins with rubber tops; sand paper on wood that makes a scratchy sound when two pieces are rubbed together.

Small bodies need to stretch, move, and dance. Young children love dancing games where they move or touch one part of their bodies on command, but they also like to dance freely to lively music. These activities help them learn rhythm, balance, and the possibilities of their own bodies. Music and dance should be a built-in part of the center's daily program.

The Staff

The equipment and materials in a preschool classroom are important, but it is the teachers who will set the tone for how they are used and for what activities. This parent explained:

It's the teachers who really related to the kids, so it's not only the center and the director. I think it's pretty important that you really like the teacher and think the kids will be comfortable. When I was first looking for child care, I noticed that the teacher didn't know much English and she really couldn't understand the kids and they couldn't understand her. So it's not only the owner but who the teachers will be—and you really have to talk to them.

Try to watch and listen to the way teachers interact with children. Notice how activities are presented, whether the teachers encourage the children's curiosity and help them to have fun while they acquire new skills.

Do the teachers:
- give children choices about what they want to do?
- help them find what they need?

- encourage children to explore materials in their own way, at their own pace?
- sit with the children while they work, using the materials themselves, or talking with the children about what they are doing?
- explain ideas and concepts in language that is understandable to young children?
- give boys and girls the same opportunities for participation in all activities? Do they encourage girls to work in the block area? Boys to do art work?
- react with enthusiasm to children's discoveries and accomplishments?
- encourage children to do their own problem solving?
- offer assistance when needed?
- help the children to work cooperatively with one another?

Good preschool teachers do not remain aloof from the children and their activities. They need to be comfortable using the finger paints themselves, dancing with the children, getting down on the floor to play. A mother describes one such teacher:

When Tina started day care, she was having a little trouble separating from me. I'll never forget the day we walked in and saw the teacher down on all fours playing train. He was the engine and all the kids were latching on to one another behind him, moving around the room and making train noises. Tina took one look and said, "I want to be a train too." She told me to go to work. He was so good at setting up a situation that was inviting and fun because he was relaxed and having a good time in the game himself.

Three- and four-year-old children are usually social beings. They enjoy being with their peers and take the business of making and keeping friends very seriously. However, they are still self-centered in many ways. Part of the importance of the preschool experience is to help them learn to balance their own needs with those of a group. Being in a group is a lot of fun, but it is also hard work for a young child. Good teachers are skilled in creating an environment and a schedule that helps preschoolers manage this task. They do this by:

- *having realistic expectations of young children:* gearing activities to short attention spans; selecting materials that match the skill levels of the age group; alternating active times with quiet times; making sure children get individual attention.

- *setting limits that are consistent and appropriate:* establishing guidelines for safety and enforcing them; keeping children from hurting one another by quick intervention, and modeling appropriate ways to deal with anger; making sure that there are adequate materials and that children have opportunities to try different activities; applying rules consistently and calmly.
- *valuing each child as an individual:* recognizing the different strengths of each child and accentuating these; knowing who needs extra encouragement and providing it; helping the children to see individual differences in a positive way; providing opportunities for children to work cooperatively together and make friends.

A preschooler's day should include times to be with the whole group —meals, stories, music, meetings—as well as times to play individually or in small groups. There should be periods for outdoor play, when children can exercise, run, climb, and be noisy. And there should be times for quiet activities where children are focusing their attention on particular tasks.

A good schedule should look something like this:

> morning activity period
> snack time
> circle time—meeting, story, and/or music activities
> outdoor play
> lunch
> rest time
> afternoon activity period
> snack
> outdoor time
> circle time

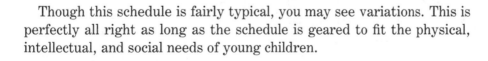

Though this schedule is fairly typical, you may see variations. This is perfectly all right as long as the schedule is geared to fit the physical, intellectual, and social needs of young children.

Observe Key Interactions

Teachers need a great deal of skill to help young children adapt to moving from one activity to another. Observe how the teachers handle transition periods like the following:

Arrival and Departure

If you can get to the center early in the morning, you will have a good opportunity to see what kind of rapport teachers and parents have. You will also be able to observe the teachers' skill in helping children make the sometimes difficult transition from home to school. Late in the afternoon is another good time to see how the children like the program; as this mother noticed:

Lots of times when I go to pick my child up, he doesn't want to go home and that's comforting to me because I know he's really enjoying himself. I notice the same thing with other parents, who have to stand back and argue back and forth with their kid. But I'd rather see that than come in and see my child crying. This way I feel I'm getting my money's worth.

Notice if teachers:
- have the room set up and ready when families arrive.
- give a warm greeting to each arriving child.
- help children find an activity or playmate.
- make sure parents say goodbye directly to their children when they are leaving.
- offer physical and verbal reassurance if a child is sad.

Snacks and Meals

Eating times should be pleasant and give children the chance to interact with their friends and their teachers.

Notice whether:
- children are involved in setting up, serving, and cleaning up.
- teachers sit with the children while they eat.
- food is served in an appetizing way.
- hot food is served hot.
- children get enough to eat.
- utensils are clean.
- children can sit with their friends at snack and meals.
- conversation is encouraged.

You should NOT see children:

- forced to eat.
- sitting at tables for a long time waiting to be served.
- eating without adult supervision.
- running around with food in their mouth.
- denied snacks or dessert as a punishment or given as a reward.

Group Times

Circle time gives the children a chance to get together as a group for meetings, stories, and music, and it should be built into the daily schedule. Skilled teachers will select discussion topics, books, and musical activities that are fun and that encourage kids to participate.

Notice whether teachers:

- have chosen topics, stories, or games that seem to interest the children.
- are flexible about changing the plan if it isn't working.
- encourage the children to participate.
- avoid forcing any child to participate by putting him on the spot.
- try to help a child who is having a hard time participating or is being disruptive, by sitting next to her or giving her a special job to do.

Handling Disputes or Aggressive Behavior

Teachers must often act as mediators when young children have disagreements. Frequently, these fights occur over particular toys or equipment. Though three- and four-year-olds are ready to learn about taking turns and sharing, the adults must make sure that things really are shared and promised turns do come. When disputes arise, teachers should protect children from physical harm and show them there are other ways to negotiate disagreements.

Notice if teachers:

- intervene quickly if children are physically or verbally abusing each other.
- listen to each child's explanation of what happened.
- help the aggressor, as well as the victim, work out the dispute.

- encourage the children to use words to express their feelings to each other.
- model appropriate behavior by treating their co-workers with respect and relating in a friendly manner.

You should NOT see:

- teachers involved in long discussions with each other and not supervising the children.
- any physical punishment of a child by a teacher under any circumstances.
- children shouted at or otherwise verbally abused.
- children isolated from the group—told to face the wall or sit in their cubby or sent out in the hall.
- children told they are "bad." It is important that teachers make it clear that they are criticizing particular *behavior*, not making a judgment about the individual child.

This mother removed her child from a center precisely because of this type of attitude:

When I started working full-time, I really needed good child care. A city agency referred me to a day care center, so I took my son there. I wasn't that comfortable with it, but I was totally desperate. I didn't like the feeling of the classroom. There was a kind of hostility to the children, that basically a good child did this, that and the other, and if you didn't, you must be bad. I got a little suspicious when my kid would come home with grease stains on his clothes. When I asked where they came from, he said, "Well, they were trying to force-feed me because I'm a vegetarian." I didn't know what to do . . . I didn't know any other place to take him. And then after two weeks I was walking in to pick my son up and I heard two children just crying their hearts out and some woman just jabbering away at the top of her lungs. And I come to find out one of the kids was my son. The two of them had been running around and had bumped into each other and knocked their heads and were crying. And she was screaming her head off at them and telling me how awful he was. So I said, "You won't have to worry about this anymore," and I took my son and walked out.

Consoling and Comforting

Early childhood is a time of hurt feelings and hurt knees. It is also a time when children need prompt and gentle comfort.

You should see teachers:

- respond quickly when a child is injured or unhappy.
- provide physical comfort—a hug, a lap, a hand to hold—when needed.
- listen sympathetically to the child's feelings.

You should NOT see:

- children told they are "too big to cry."
- children left alone when they are unhappy.
- children made fun of in front of their peers.

Sometimes the need for consolation and comfort goes beyond the day-to-day skirmishes of classroom life. Three- and four-year-olds are sensitive to things they hear about in the world around them. They are often scared about robbers, fires, the idea of their parents separating, or whether they might be "replaced" by the birth of a sibling. At this age, many children begin to ponder serious questions. Preschool teachers are frequently asked such questions as: "Where do people come from?" "What happens when they die?" "Is Santa Claus real?" What teachers say about any of these issues is taken very seriously by the children in their care. Children think a teacher, like a parent, knows it all. It is essential that those who are caring for children of this age have the maturity, sensitivity, and tact to handle these topics thoughtfully. A parent describes a situation that required these qualities:

When my little boy was four, the classroom pet, a guinea pig, kicked the bucket. When the children got to school and found out, they were very upset, but the teacher was great. She gathered them together and talked about their sadness, telling them that is how people usually feel when a person or animal dies. She read them a wonderful book about how everything changes in its own time. Then she told them that the best way to help with their sadness was to think about all the happy things they could remember about Max. They made a chart, with each child saying something special about the guinea pig. And when the kids decided that's what they wanted to do, they got a shoe box, went to the park, and buried the animal. They even had a little celebration there and left a marker and a flower on the spot. This was my son's first experience with death, and I think the teacher really handled the whole thing so well.

Managing Routines

Though it is sometimes hard for young children to conform to a daily routine, for a child care center to function, eating, drinking, and resting are usually done at specific times.

You should see:

- a morning and afternoon snack time with food and juice served calmly and cheerfully.
- lunch served before children are too tired to enjoy it. There should be flexibility. Those who finish quickly should be allowed to move on to looking at stories or another quiet activity, while the slower eaters have ample time to finish at their own pace.
- children allowed to use the toilet or get a drink of water whenever they need to.
- children assisted in dressing or undressing when necessary. Getting sweaters, jackets, and boots on and off can be an arduous task for three-year-olds. Getting ready to go outside takes time with a large group. Children who are ready first should have something to do (sing songs, look at books) until the others catch up.
- toileting accidents handled in a calm and supportive way. It can be embarrassing but not at all infrequent for a young child to wet her pants. Teachers should change the clothes promptly, reassuring the child that it's no big deal and discouraging any teasing if it starts.

Rest Time

It is unlikely that you will be observing at rest time, so make sure you find out how it is handled.

How does nap begin? Do children have some time to look at books or play quiet games by themselves on their cots? Can they rest with a stuffed animal brought from home or provided by the center? Do teachers sing lullabies or play records or tapes? Do they sit with individual children who are having a hard time falling asleep?

How long are children expected to rest or sleep? What happens if a child can't fall asleep? Must she stay on the cot? If so, for how long? Can she have a book or quiet toy after a certain amount of time? Are the cots or mats clean? Is there enough space for all the cots or mats? Does each child have her own sheet and cover? Is the room dark and quiet enough for sleeping?

Rest period can be an anxious time for young children. Teachers often take their breaks while children are resting. Find out how the scheduling works. Is a familiar adult present in the room throughout nap time?

Getting the Full Picture

Tour the Entire Facility

Is the building well maintained? Is it clean? Is it safe? Are there fire extinguishers and smoke detectors? Are radiators and pipes covered? Are there window guards? Are all hazardous substances, like cleaning fluids and pet foods, out of reach of the children? Are electric sockets covered? Is wiring out of the way? Is there any paint peeling from the walls? Is there more than one exit in case of fire?

Visit Other Classrooms

If your child will be entering the program as a three-year-old, spend a little time observing the four-year-old room as well, so you will know what kind of equipment is available and whether there is consistency in the style of teaching.

Look at the Kitchen

If meals are prepared at the center, take a good look at the kitchen. Is it clean? Is the food fresh? Any evidence of roaches, ants, or mice? Who does the cooking? What is the menu? Do the children get a full meal for lunch—meat, chicken, or fish, vegetables, starches, milk? Are parents told the menus in advance, so they can plan other meals accordingly? What kinds of snacks are served and how often? Are there fresh fruit, crackers, peanut butter, cheese? Are sweets (cookies, candy, cake, ice cream) served? If so, how frequently?

Look at the Outdoor Facilities

If there is an outdoor play space, inspect it. What kind of equipment is there? Are the slides, swings, seesaws, jungle gyms in good repair and safe? Is the playground surfaced with rubber, sand, or grass? Is the area large enough for children to run around and ride on tricycles with-

out hitting equipment or each other? If the center does not have its own outdoor facilities, ask where the children go to play. Do they go out every day? How do they get to the play area? Go with the group or later, to see what the playground or park is like. Is it in a safe place? Can the teacher keep track of the children easily? Look at the playground equipment with the same questions you would apply to the center's equipment.

Talk with the Director

The director usually sets the tone for the program and hires and supervises the staff. It's important that you feel comfortable talking about your concerns with this person. Use your time to discuss what you have observed and ask about the parts of the day you haven't seen. Do not hesitate to ask any question that is on your mind. In order to make a good decision, you need the fullest possible picture of life at the center. Make sure to find out about the following:

- How long has the center been open?
- How long have the current teachers been with the program?
- What are the qualifications of the teaching staff?
- Is there ongoing training and supervision?
- Will the teacher you observed be with your child?
- What is the maximum number of children in each group?
- What is the usual staff-child ratio? If a teacher is absent, is he replaced by another adult? What is the minimum number of adults who will be on duty at any point in the day?
- When is the center closed for short holidays or extended vacations?

Discuss Health and Safety Issues

- Find out the center's evacuation plans in the event of fire or other emergencies. Do they have routine fire drills?
- Does anyone on the staff have training in first aid?
- Is there a well-equipped first-aid kit?
- What hospital emergency room or physician is used if a child needs immediate medical attention?

■ What is the center's policy about illness? Under what circumstances would you be expected to keep your child home or pick him up because of illness? If your child is vomiting, running a fever, or has any kind of rash, he should definitely not go to the center. He should be free of fever for one full day before returning to the program. If your child exhibits any of these symptoms while at the center, you should be called. In the event of any accidents involving injury to the head, possible sprains, broken bones, or anything more serious than a minor scrape or bruise, you should be notified immediately.

The center should maintain health records on every child. You should be asked to have your doctor examine your child and fill out a complete medical form before he enters the program. You will probably be asked to sign a consent form allowing the staff to take your child to the hospital in an emergency situation. However, you should make it clear that you would expect to be notified immediately should any such situation arise.

The center should also keep up-to-date records on whom to contact in an emergency. Make sure to provide both parents' work numbers, the pediatrician's number, and the names and numbers of two friends or relatives who can be contacted in an emergency if neither parent can be reached. This should all be done prior to the time you leave your child in the center.

■ Are you welcome at the center at any time? *Do not leave your child in any program where you are told there is a policy that prohibits you from having access to your child during any part of the day.*

Make very clear who has permission to pick up your child. *The center should never release your child to anyone other than the designated people unless you have notified the staff directly about a change.* Work out how you will identify yourself if you call to make a change. The procedure should be that you state the name of the person who will be coming. Make sure the teacher who will be on duty at that time will get the message. Talk to your child as well, or ask the teacher to let your child know who is coming in your place so she won't be confused at pickup time.

Ask about the Role of Parents

Find out what the center expects from you as a parent and what kind of input you will have about the program.

If you have a free morning or afternoon, can you help out in the classroom?

Are there regularly scheduled parent meetings and parent-teacher conferences?

Will you be expected to participate in fund-raising events, clean-up days, or other activities?

Make sure to ask what fees you are expected to pay and when they are due. Payment policies vary from center to center. You may be asked to pay weekly, monthly, by semester, or in some other incremental amounts. You may be asked to sign an enrollment contract. Review this carefully. It should clearly set forth your financial responsibilities. Is a deposit required? Are refunds possible under any circumstances? What are your obligations if you decide to withdraw your child from the program? Are there any additional costs beyond the tuition, such as fees for snacks, art materials or other supplies?

Making a Decision

Think over what you have seen and heard. If you have negative feelings about the teachers, the program, or the environment, look elsewhere. If you have further questions, ask them. If you feel you need to visit again or have your spouse visit, ask whether this can be arranged.

The single most important factor in your decision should be your feelings about the teaching staff. Did you like them? Are they the role models you want for your child? Will you feel comfortable talking to them if problems arise? Was the size of the group appropriate? Were there enough teachers for the number of children in the group?

Did the children seem happy and well cared for? Would your child enjoy the kinds of activities you saw? Did the daily schedule seem appropriate? Try to visualize your child in the group. Is it a happy image? Trust your instincts. You are the best judge of what your child needs.

Prepare Your Child in Advance

It is a good idea to begin talking about the program with your child about a month before her starting date. If she has been in a family day care home or with an in-home caregiver, you need to help her bring closure to this arrangement and prepare for something new.

Talk in very concrete and positive terms about what the center is like. Tell her about specific toys that she may be familiar with from home: "They have Lego bricks just like yours, and some of our favorite books." Mention, too, some new and exciting things that you saw on your visit: "They have a bunny rabbit whose name is Funny Bunny and a toy stove for cooking." Talk about the teachers by name, what they look like, and the activities they do with the children.

Take some cues from your child's reactions: If she has lots of questions answer them, but don't overload her with too much information all at once if she seems disinterested or anxious. Mention things about the center when it seems appropriate. For instance, if you are out in a playground, tell her what the center's play yard is like. You may want to take her for a visit, but check first whether the teacher and children she will see would in fact be there when she comes; otherwise, the visit may be confusing. It's important to let your child know that you will take her to the center and spend time while she is getting to know her teachers and new friends.

Getting Started

Even if your child has been in some kind of child care situation before, the first few days or weeks at an early childhood center require special attention. There's a new place to adjust to, new children and adults to meet, a new routine—to say nothing of the anxiety some children experience at this separation from their parents. You, too, may very well be feeling anxious about the impending separation. This teacher describes her own observations of parents and children in these circumstances:

As a preschool teacher, I often had to be more attentive to the parent than to the child when the parent had to leave. I'd say, "I really know that you feel very bad about leaving. Is there someone else the child is comfortable with that could stay?" If there wasn't, we would tell them they should try to get back in a little while. It caused a lot of stress, because some parents really have to leave and can't come back before the end of the day. That's tough on parents *and* the kids.

Kids do best when the parents and the teachers have a lot going together as a team. But all children, even the four- and five-year-olds, at the beginning of the year, they still want to see their parents around. I never worked in a preschool classroom that didn't permit some kind of phasing out of parent presence. And I'd never let my own child go to a program that didn't do that.

It may be hard to take time off from work to be with your child during this period, but it will be worth it. Generally speaking, kids whose parents help them settle into a new center do better than those who are left too abruptly.

Early childhood programs have different ways of dealing with this adjustment period. Some will ask that you bring your child only for a few hours during the first few days. Others begin with a full-day schedule. Almost all centers, however, should ask you to stay with your child *at least* the first day.

The policy of most centers is based on experience and an understanding of what helps children make a good adjustment. Your own instincts and the cues you get from your child are, however, of great importance. Figure out what's best for your child and talk with the teacher about it. You may decide to come in for a couple of hours every day for the first week. You may want to spend one or two full days going through the daily routine.

Good centers will usually be somewhat flexible, since they realize that it is to everyone's advantage for things to go smoothly. During the adjustment period, it will be most helpful to your child if you can assist her in forming a relationship with at least one staff member in the room. She will, of course, get to know everyone in time, but initially she will do best if there is one adult she feels she can trust. Good teachers are very sensitive to how each child is reacting during the first few days and will adapt their approach to what might work best for an individual child, as this mother describes:

The first few days at the center, Casey would fling herself on the floor outside the classroom door, cry, and refuse to enter the room. After a few mornings of this routine, one of the teachers came out of the room and lay down on the floor beside her. She got her involved in conversation and within minutes they were giggling together. Casey went into the room with her and from then on she had a good time.

In addition to spending time at the center there are other ways to help ease your child's adjustment:

- Make sure to bring whatever your child needs—blanket, sheet, any special animal, doll, or other security object he is used to having for naps.
- When you leave, make sure you say goodbye directly to your child and the teacher. Tell them both when you will be back. Since young children usually cannot tell time, give a concrete guideline, such as, "After you come back from the playground," or "When Mary says it is six o'clock." *Never sneak out the door while your child is occupied. It may make her sad to see you go, but handling separation is an important learning experience. If she doesn't know when you are leaving, it is likely to make her hesitant to get involved in the activities for fear you won't be there when she looks up.*
- Make sure to come back when you said you would.

Some children have a very hard time adjusting in the first few days or weeks. Others may let you go with little fuss and, perhaps a few weeks or even months later, have a very hard time saying goodbye. Some kids seem to adjust quickly and with relatively few problems. Although it's always difficult to leave a crying child, it's important to keep in mind that managing separation is part of the growing process. But it's essential that when you do leave your child, you feel very confident that the teacher will provide the emotional and physical support that's needed. When your child can share his sadness and be comforted, it is the beginning of a solid bond between him and his teacher.

Parent-Teacher Relationships

Your child will do best at the center if you and the teachers develop a good, supportive relationship.

- Make sure to bring your child and pick her up at the scheduled times. When children come late in the morning, it is hard for teachers to greet them and help them get settled because they are already enmeshed in the morning's activities.
- If you arrive late for pickup, your child will certainly feel anxious and the teachers may feel resentful—just the way you would if you were unexpectedly detained at your job. Here's the point of view of an experienced teacher:

I worked in day care, and parents don't realize that when they are supposed to be there at a certain time, they really should be. If you're late, that not only affects the teacher, but the child knows. Even though the child is too young to tell time by the clock, he can tell time by the sun and he knows his mother is supposed to pick him up when the sun goes down. When it gets dark, the child gets panicky.

- Leave a little time in the mornings to help your child get settled, and be prepared to spend a few minutes at the end of the day helping her to say goodbye. You may rush in, tired from a day at work and anxious to get home. Yet young children often don't want to leave too quickly. They've waited for you, and now that you're there, they may want to take their time. If you can manage to leave a little transition time on most days, your child will probably be amenable on days when you really are in a hurry.
- Find out from the teachers whether there are ways you can be helpful —accompanying the group on a trip, contributing supplies, providing a special snack.
- Attend parent meetings and parent-teacher conferences. Ask your questions, raise your concerns, make suggestions.
- If things are going well, make sure to let the teachers know you are pleased. Sometimes we take good care for granted and only stop to talk when we have a complaint. It's important for the teachers to know that their work is appreciated.
- Keep the teachers informed about events going on in your child's life that may affect his classroom behavior. If there is stress of some sort in the family—the impending birth of a sibling, a hospitalized parent, the death of a family pet—it's important for the staff to know so they can be helpful.

This parent prepared well for a health problem:

When we found out my little boy had to have a hernia operation, I told his teachers how I was explaining it to him and asked them to tell me if he made any comments at school. The day of the operation, we had just walked in the door of our apartment when the phone rang. It was the center director. She said they had all been thinking about Luke and wanted to know how things went. She told me not to worry about his return to the center. If he was restricted in his activities for a few weeks and couldn't go play on the roof, they would arrange for him to do something special with a staff member downstairs so he wouldn't feel bad. Her support was great.

If Problems Arise

If you have been careful in your selection and helped your child make a good adjustment to the center, things will probably go well. This doesn't mean that your child will necessarily bounce out of bed each morning, anxious to rush off to school. Life doesn't always run smoothly for anybody—including preschool children. Sometimes a reprimand from a teacher or a problem with a friend can cause a child to say she doesn't want to go to school. If your child has been ill or on vacation, spending time at home with you, she may be reluctant to go back to school and give up that special attention. Sometimes children, like grown-ups, simply feel bored by the same routine and want a day off. The Minnesota father in the following story had an interesting approach to the daily grind:

Once when I picked my little boy up from day care he said, "Dad, when can I have a vacation?" He wanted to stay home and not do anything, just like a vacation day for older people. So we did. We picked a day and stayed home and played hooky together.

If your child expresses negative feelings about going to the center for more than a day or two, definitely talk with the teacher about what may have triggered the feelings. In most cases, problems are fairly easily solved. However, if your child is consistently unhappy, or afraid of school, and you cannot discover why and resolve the problem, you will need to consider finding a different program. This situation will be discussed in Chapter 11, "Changing Child Care Arrangements."

EARLY CHILDHOOD PROGRAMS: CHECKLIST

Name of program _____ Date visited _____

BASIC INFORMATION	Yes	No
Program is licensed	___	___
Hours are suitable	___	___
Fees are affordable	___	___

GENERAL ATMOSPHERE	Yes	No
Setting is bright and cheerful	___	___
Building is safe and well maintained	___	___
Children seem happy	___	___

THE STAFF	Yes	No
There are enough teachers to give children individual attention	___	___
Teachers respond promptly when children need assistance	___	___
Teachers have a good rapport with children and parents	___	___
Teachers participate in activities with children	___	___
Teachers set good health and safety limits	___	___
The director is accessible and responsive	___	___

THE PROGRAM	Yes	No
There is a balanced daily schedule	___	___
Activities are varied and age-appropriate	___	___
Children play outdoors each day	___	___
Boys and girls are equally encouraged to participate in activities	___	___

The following materials are available to children:
art supplies ___ blocks ___ manipulative toys ___ books ___ sand/water/clay ___ music ___

PARENT INVOLVEMENT	Yes	No
There are scheduled parent meetings	___	___
There are parent-teacher conferences	___	___
Parents are welcome to spend time at the center	___	___

COMMENTS

Child Care for School-age Children

"*T*he kids' father was able to stay with them when they were very young because he had a weird schedule. Then when they were five and seven and going into school, we had our first child care experience. It did not dawn on me until right then that school got out at one time and I got off work at another time."

It is not unusual for parents to think that when their children get to elementary school, the family's child care worries will be over. Unfortunately, a child's entrance into school only brings a new set of problems for parents who work full-time. The kind of arrangements you made previously were probably built around your schedule at work. Most likely you had one individual, in your home or hers, or a child care center that covered the hours you needed. But child care for school-age children is a new ball game.

Now you have to plan around a school schedule. You may need care in the early mornings, if you have to be at work before school opens, and care in the late afternoons. There will be vacations, and random days when school is closed and your office isn't. It isn't a simple problem. It's often harder to find part-time child care than full-time—and to locate someone or some place that will be at your beck and call for a day here and a week there is very difficult. Many thousands of parents face this situation, and unfortunately, the demand for school-age child care is a lot greater than what's available.

Planning around a complicated schedule is not the only challenge you face. As a child gets older, she will want, indeed insist on, taking part in the plans you make. For your five-, six- or seven-year-old it will probably be best, if you can find it, to have a consistent arrangement to cover all or most of the time you're away. But by eight or nine, your child will have clear and definite feelings about where she wants to go and whom she's going with. Kids often want to do different things on different days, and that frequently involves what their friends are doing. The child may begin to demand greater independence, balking at the idea of too much structure—even at the idea that she needs child care at all. If you don't include your children in the planning, they will almost certainly give you a hard time. This mother assumed it would be best for her children if she could pick them up herself, and was very surprised by their reaction:

Both my kids would stay at a woman's house in the neighborhood, but I didn't feel right about it. I got into a more flexible job situation, so I could pick the kids up after school myself and take care of them. My son got real angry with me because he couldn't go and play with all the other kids, and I'm thinking, But I've arranged my life so we could be together!

You'll need flexibility and creative thinking to make a workable plan and you may find yourself with a patchwork of arrangements. You may have to rely on family members and friends to cover the early morning and the times when school is closed for a day or an extended vacation. You may find a good after-school program, or it may work best for you to cover the afternoons with a combination of music lessons, sports clubs, religious school, etc.—assuming your child is old enough to get to these places on his own or that there is someone to take him.

The cost will be another important factor. This California mother is trying to cope with that problem:

The cost has been shocking to me. I have two children, and when I start thinking about what it's going to take to care for these kids . . . After-school care, for instance, would be $350 a month for each one, and during the summer it would be $400 for full-time care for a school-age child. So it isn't going down. It's really scary, because you hear the teachers are not making enough money to support themselves and their families, and on the other hand, there are the parents who can't afford to pay that much money either. So what do you do?

Depending on where you live and your children's ages, you may have several options or very few. Some of the possibilities to explore are:

Care at the School

Because so many parents are concerned about the issue of "latchkey" children, many communities have been organizing to develop services. The schools themselves seem an obvious option, and in many areas elementary schools are providing early-morning and late-afternoon programs. Sometimes they provide afternoon care when school is only open for a half-day and full-time care during vacations. This trend is likely to continue, and expanded school hours may well provide a good solution for many working parents. In some cases, the local school systems are administering these programs. Most often, however, they are operated by local community organizations. Although they use school space, these programs are run independently, with their own administrative and child care staff. They almost always charge a fee.

If such a program is not available at your child's school, you may want to work with other parents to convince the school to get one started. Parent power can be one of your best resources for getting what you need.

Programs Away from School

If a school program is not an option, there may be an after-school center near your child's school. These are generally run by community groups such as YMCAs, girls' and boys' clubs, churches, synagogues, and day care centers. They may also be run by companies whose business is child care. Some of these programs also provide full-time vacation care, on days when school is closed.

If you are lucky, the program will offer a pickup service from your child's school. Depending on the distance involved, this may mean a bus or car service or an adult escort, who will meet your child at his school and walk him to the after-school center. If there isn't such a service, find out if other children from your child's school will be using the same program. If there is a large enough group, the center may be willing to provide a pickup or to advise you on how other families have coped. Perhaps an older, responsible child from the same school, a student teacher, a clerical worker, or a parent who isn't working would be interested in the job of escorting your child to the program.

Specialized Programs and Clubs

Some afternoon programs offer specific activities on different days of the week: Monday—gymnastics; Tuesday—drama; Wednesday—art. These activities, usually supervised by specialists, may take place at nonprofit community organizations or at profit-making facilities. There are also afternoon programs with a particular focus, similar to a club. They offer only sports, only arts activities, or only music. It's often possible to enroll your child for specific afternoons. Although you can certainly use these programs for child care coverage, they may not be set up to fully meet the needs of parents who work full-time. The hours may be shorter than those an after-school program provides and they will probably not offer full-time care during school vacation periods. If you only need care on certain days, if your child is really interested in pursuing specific activities, and if there is some way to get her there, this may be an option to consider.

Family Day Care

Family day care, in the caregiver's home, usually is geared to younger children. Many providers, however, take school-age children for the early morning or late hours of the day and some can provide full-time care on days when school is closed. In this kind of arrangement, the parent takes the child to the provider in the early morning and, if necessary, the provider takes the child to school. In the afternoons, the provider may pick up the child at school and care for him until one of the parents arrives from work. (See Chapter 5 for detailed information on family day care providers.)

Part-time Care in Your Home

If late afternoons are a problem, you may want to look for someone who will pick up your child at school or meet him at the school bus, take him to your home, and provide supervision until you get back. An option that may save you money and give the child some companionship is to get together with another family or two to hire a caregiver. In this shared-care arrangement, you can use one home or rotate the care at different homes on a weekly or monthly basis.

College or graduate students, particularly those studying education, may be interested in the kind of hours you are offering. Check with the job-placement services of local colleges and universities. You also may be able to find a mature and reliable high school student. Often their school days are as long or longer than elementary school hours, but sometimes it works out:

When my daughter started kindergarten, there was no after-school. I had no idea what I was going to do, none. I mean, there was no one in the neighborhood who could help. So there I am, registering her, sitting in the office at the school. A few other parents were there, talking and waiting for papers to be processed, and I'm saying, "Gee, I don't know what I'm going to do." Well, one parent said, "I have a daughter in her senior year of high school, and she has to watch her brother. Would you want to meet her and think about sharing the care?" And that's what happened.

Sometimes retired people are interested in part-time employment. You can post notices in your neighborhood or inquire at senior-citizen centers and local community organizations.

If you need early-morning care as well, your task will be harder. The part-time person you find may be able to do it, but few people are interested in such a split shift of hours. More likely, you'll need to improvise. Perhaps one parent or the other can make an adjustment in work hours, or you can arrange with a neighbor or your older child to cover the mornings.

If you've had a caregiver providing full-time care in your home up to this point or feel you need someone to help with the housework as well as provide child care, you may want to consider an in-home caregiver to coordinate after-school arrangements and provide coverage when school is closed or your child is ill. (See Chapter 4 for detailed information on

in-home caregivers.) This arrangement can be expensive, but especially if you also have a younger child at home, it is often the most practical solution.

Utilizing Family and Friends

People in your family or friends who are not working may be a good resource for part-time child care. Your mother or mother-in-law might enjoy this special, relatively short time with her grandchild. If your brother, sister, or good friend is at home in the afternoons with his or her own child, that person might be willing to take care of your child too. Depending on the situation and the nature of your relationship, it may or may not be appropriate to make a financial arrangement. Many families find that in situations where a payment agreement can be worked out tactfully, the arrangement is more dependable over an extended period of time and there is less likelihood of resentment on either side. For some families it's an ideal plan:

I started going to work when my kids were five and seven years old. It was easy because our relatives were right next door. We could run out of the house, run next door, then jump in the car and go.

Families and friends are often the best resource available for those random days when school is closed and for covering extended school vacations. Many parents also rotate with spouses, relatives, or friends to take some time off so nobody has to miss too many days at work.

Care by Older Siblings

If you have a teenager, you may need him to take care of a younger sibling. If you are considering this arrangement, it may be helpful to think about the following:

- Is your older child interested in taking on the job, or would you have to persuade or order him to do it?
- How do the two children get along? Do they have a good rapport, or do they quarrel often?
- When you've left them alone in other situations, how did it work out?

- Would you pay the older child or offer some other kind of compensation?
- Is he reliable? Absentminded? Competent to handle emergencies?
- How much would the arrangement cut into your older child's social life, time for homework, sports, or other activities?
- Would your younger child accept supervision from an older sibling?
- Would you allow the older child to have friends over? If so, would he still focus attention on his child care responsibilities? Would the younger child's presence annoy him? Would the little one be excluded? Neglected? Involved in inappropriate activities?
- Would your younger child be able to invite friends over? Is your teenager willing and able to take on the additional responsibility of supervising other kids?
- Would you feel comfortable letting your children go out, or would you want them to stay home?

Parents generally say that this kind of arrangement works best if they do not rely on it exclusively. If your younger child takes a gymnastics or music class one or two days a week or has a regular play date at a friend's house, this would allow the older child some free afternoons. It's best, if you can do it, to give both children time to do what they enjoy so they won't resent their time together.

Self-care

I'd feel okay leaving my daughter alone at home for a while. She's eight, going on nine.

My biggest horror story was when my son was home alone. He was turning on the water and the faucets broke. The water started spouting all over, so he went down to the basement. He thought he was turning off the water, but he turned on the gas. I thought I had prepared him for all those things, but I never thought about showing him the water and the gas in the basement.

We live in a private home and I would not feel comfortable with the two of them ever being there alone—until they are twenty-one and twenty-three! I did leave them one morning to come to a conference. I woke them up and I said, "Mommy is going to work and Daddy will be here within an hour." I felt fine until I saw a program on television where a woman had left home just to take her husband to the train station, like five minutes away from home, and she came back and all three of her kids were . . . there had been an electrical-circuit fire or something, and they were dead.

There are some children you can leave alone pretty young, and there are some you may never be able to. I did a lot of preparing to leave my daughter, so she was familiar with keys and the phone and that was very normal to her at a very early age. A lot depends on the neighborhood and the building you live in and how you feel about them getting from school to home.

I think one of the things I feel most guilty about when I think back is my own strong memories of coming home from school and my mother greeting me and having something special for me to eat. Well, when Sara got to be high-school age, I told her that's one thing I feel guilty about, and she said, "I loved coming home alone! I could eat what I wanted to and I liked that quiet time all by myself." I guess it didn't do any permanent damage to her.

If you have very few options or if your child is balking at the idea of after-school care, you may find yourself considering the idea of letting her stay alone at home in the afternoon. It is probably not a good idea to let a child under the age of nine stay by herself under any circumstances, but age is not the only indicator of a child's readiness for this responsibility. A lot has to do with how mature your child is, how comfortable you would feel with such an arrangement, how safe your neighborhood is, and what kind of support system would be available. Although staying alone may work for a particular child, it is a situation with potential problems. If this seems like the only option you have, it may be helpful to consider the following questions:

- How has your child done when left alone for short periods of time? Was she scared? Comfortable? Did she find things to occupy her time? How would she feel after dark?
- Have you instructed her on what to do in emergency situations? A fire? An accident? An intruder?
- Is there a neighbor nearby who is always home during the hours your child would be alone? Would she be willing to come to your child's aid if there was a problem? Does your child know how to reach the neighbor? Would she feel comfortable doing so?
- Would your child be responsible about keeping track of the house key and locking the door?

- Is she able to use the telephone? Does she know where you work? Your phone numbers and extensions?
- Does she know about dialing 911 or your local emergency number and in what situations it's appropriate?
- Do you have a list of emergency phone numbers by the phone—the doctor, hospital, police, poison-control center? If she needed to call these numbers, would she know what to say to get help?
- Would she know what to do if someone came to the door? What to say or not say when strangers telephone?
- Would you allow her to play outside in the yard, ride her bike on the street, go to the park or playground? Does she know the safety precautions she should take? Have you discussed how she should respond if approached by a stranger? Do you feel she might be gullible to the ploys of an adult, or stick carefully to the guidelines you have given her?
- Do you have the kind of job where your child could reach you easily? Could you leave if you needed to? Could you get home in less than twenty minutes or contact a reliable adult to go to the house immediately in case of an emergency?
- If you would be leaving two children alone, with neither old enough to be in charge, how would they get along? Would they be supportive of one another or more likely to get into trouble? Would they quarrel?

These are just some of the issues to keep in mind. If you are seriously considering this type of arrangement, it will probably be helpful to contact the people at Project Home Safe (see resource section, page 201). They will send you free materials to help you evaluate whether your child is mature enough to stay by herself, as well as information on preparing her for the responsibility.

There are a number of books to help parents and kids manage a self-care arrangement. Some that have been suggested by Project Home Safe are: *School's Out—Now What? Creative Choices for Your Child,* by Joan Bergstrom, Ten Speed Press, 1984; *The Handbook for Latchkey Children and Their Parents,* by Lynette and Thomas Long, Priam Books, 1983; *Home Alone Kids: the Working Parent's Guide to Providing the Best Care for Your Child,* by Bryan Robinson, Robbie Rowland, and Mick Coleman, Lexington Books, 1989.

Finding School-age Child Care

If you have access to a child care resource and referral agency (see page 203), the counselors will be able to tell you what types of care are available. They will give you information about costs and local regulations and refer you to specific programs and services. If you do not have access to such a group, talk to the principal or secretary at your child's school for suggestions. You can also contact community YMCAs, churches, synagogues, girls' and boys' clubs, and the Police Athletic League. Check your local newspapers—child care programs often run ads at the beginning of the school year. Your local library may also have information about programs in your community.

As in most aspects of raising a child, talking with other parents who have been through the experience is likely to be one of the best ways to find good after-school care.

After-school Programs

It is best to begin contacting programs five or six months before you need them, so you can visit while the program is in operation. No other method of gathering information is as good as firsthand observation. After-school centers are usually closed during the summer or are running day camps with different staff and activities. If, however, that's the only time you can visit, it's a good idea to do so: You can at least see what the physical facilities are like.

When you have identified some programs that might meet your needs, call and get some basic information to see if it makes sense to visit:

- How many children are in the program?
- What age children does the program serve?
- Are they divided by age into separate groups?
- How many children are in each group?
- How many adults supervise?
- What kinds of activities are available?
- Do the children have choices about what activities to participate in?
- What are the qualifications of the supervising adults? Are they teachers? College students? High school students?
- What kind of training are they receiving on the job?

- Is the program open all day on days when school is closed?
- How much does the program cost? Do you pay on a weekly, monthly, or yearly basis? If your child has a prolonged illness or you leave the program, will you be able to get a refund?
- If the program is not located at your child's school, is there a pickup service? How much does it cost?
- How long has the program been running?
- Is it licensed?

Ask for a brochure or other literature, and find out the enrollment deadlines. If you are going to visit while the program is in operation, plan to spend some time speaking with the director. If you are visiting the facility during the summer and the after-school director is not there, find out when he will return. Usually, by the end of August the administrative staff of an after-school program is back at work and available to parents. Try to schedule a time to talk with the director during this period.

Government Regulation

Though there are states that include school-age child care within their licensing standards for day care centers, these regulations often cover only programs that run for more than three or four hours a day. For this reason, after-school programs are often unregulated. Some states, however, are now beginning to develop regulations for this specific age group. It's important to find out if there are regulations where you live and what they are. Bear in mind, though, that licensing regulations generally set only minimum standards. Any program you consider should *at least* meet these, but you should be an informed consumer to select a quality program.

What Should a Good After-school Program Offer?

An after-school program should not be a continuation of the school day, with the same kind of structured focus on academic activities. Nor should it be a baby-sitting service, where children just wait around with little to do until their parents are finished working.

One way to think about it is to consider what children generally like to do when they come home after school. Depending on the kind of day they've had, they may feel more or less energetic, in a good mood or a bad one. They may need some quiet time for themselves or, on other days, want to be with their friends—to talk and play in a much more relaxed way than they can at school. Many kids need to "break loose" after school. They want to be outside playing team sports, jumping rope, roller skating, playing catch.

These are the ages where children enjoy pursuing specific interests and developing new skills. Often they like to form clubs or work on special projects with other kids. Some children like to get their home-work out of the way quickly while others need a break before focusing their attention back on schoolwork.

A good after-school program should be flexible enough to accommo-date the different ages, needs, and moods of the kids, offering stimulat-ing and interesting activities but not insisting on participation. Children should have the opportunity to make choices about what they want to do.

These are the features that should be present in a quality program for school-age children:

Pleasant and Safe Physical Environment

An after-school program should take place in a facility that is clean, well ventilated, and well lit. Walls, floors, and ceilings should be in good shape, electric wiring and fixtures safe and in good repair. The kitchen should be clean, with perishable food kept refrigerated. There should be no evidence of bugs or mice. The bathrooms should be well maintained, clean, and supplied with toilet paper, soap, and paper towels. The facil-ity should have more than one clearly marked exit, fire extinguishers, and smoke detectors. There should be a clear plan for evacuation in case of fire or other emergencies and periodic practice drills. There should be good medical emergency contingency plans, as this parent points out:

The program actually was run by a reputable organization, but one incident really bothered me. My son broke his elbow at the park while I was in transit to pick him up, I found out they waited about forty-five minutes before they even made an attempt to call me at work and the counselors made a judgment to just stay at the playground instead of bringing him back immediately. I wasn't angry that he hurt himself, just at the way they handled it.

Facilities for Active Play

Most children do not get much time to exercise their large muscles during regular school hours. They have probably spent most of the day sitting and will need a chance to run around. The program should have a good outdoor space for physical activities—either on its own grounds or nearby. Some facilities may also have a large room or fully equipped gym—for basketball, tumbling, relay races. Not every center can provide so much space, and you may decide it is less important than other qualities.

Equipment in the outdoor play area should be safe—swings well attached, seesaws securely bolted—and there should be a rubber, sand, or grass surface to prevent injuries from falls. If gymnastics or swimming are offered, equipment should be safe, there should be clear rules for participation, and the supervising adults should be fully trained and qualified to teach the sport. Children should never use gymnastics equipment without a coach working with them on a one-to-one basis. Water safety is essential. A Red Cross-certified lifeguard should be on duty whenever the pool is in use. The pool should be well maintained, its bacteria level frequently checked, and showers should be available for use before and after swimming.

Space for Quiet Activities

After a day at school, children may need time alone, a quiet place to daydream, do homework, paint, or read a book. Some may want to do things with just one or two friends—play a game of checkers, Monopoly, cards, or jacks. There should be a few quiet corners in the facility to accommodate them.

Variety of Activities and Materials

An after-school program can give children a chance to do some of the same things they do at school, but in a less structured way. They may have art classes or sing in a chorus at school. They may work on computers or study drama. In an after-school program children should feel more freedom to experiment: to take an old computer apart and learn how it works; to organize a band; to write a play, make the costumes and perform their own work. An after-school program is also a place for kids to develop their athletic abilities. There should be a basketball hoop, softball equipment, a volleyball, and other sports supplies. Such skills as cooking, carpentry, sewing, or gardening can also be acquired in a good program.

Good, Nutritious Food

Children are usually hungry at the end of a school day, and the atmosphere should convey a feeling of generous plenty—though not when it comes to sweets and soft drinks. Nutritious and filling snacks like fruit, cheese, peanut butter, milk, and juice should be available. The kids may be involved in planning and preparing snacks, an easy and enjoyable way to learn about nutrition. They may sometimes go shopping with an adult to select food for their group.

Reliable and Qualified Staff

After-school programs are frequently staffed by college students, and sometimes by high school students. These young people may have done some baby-sitting or worked as camp counselors, but they probably have no formal training or experience in working with school-age children. If they are energetic and really like kids, they can have very good relationships with the children in their care and make the program seem less like school. There should, however, be ongoing training and supervision by a well-qualified director, so that the staff has the skill to handle a variety of situations and understands what kind of behavior is appropriate for children of different ages. If their expectations are unrealistic, they are likely to be critical of behavior that is perfectly normal, as this Atlanta mother's example illustrates:

When my son was a first grader and full of energy, he was in an after-school center where they wanted kids to be quiet as soon as they came into the program. I would get greeted at the door every day by somebody who would say, "Well, he really does have a difficult time settling down." And I would say, "Well, it's probably because he's in school all day."

Small Groups and Good Adult Supervision

Most school systems have relatively large classes, with one supervising teacher. In an after-school program, kids should have the opportunity to be in smaller groups. Experts suggest that for children between the ages of five and seven, there should be at least one adult for a group of ten children. For older children, a group size of thirteen with at least one adult is workable. In general, however, you're likely to have a more flexible program and individual attention with additional adult support.

Good Communication with Parents

It's important that parents feel welcome at the center and that the director and members of the staff be accessible. *Do not leave your child in any center where there is a policy prohibiting you from having access to your child at any time.*

Find out what the center expects from you and what kind of input you will have about the program and what your child is doing. It is often difficult for working parents to get very involved with an after-school program. The limited time you have available for meetings, fund-raising, and serving on parent committees will more likely be devoted to the school. Many after-school programs understand this and expect relatively little from parents in time and commitment. On the other hand, it can be difficult to feel removed from your child's daily ups and downs, as this parent describes:

When they're infants or toddlers and you feel comfortable about the caregiver, you can sort of get over that, but when they're older and looking you in your face and saying that they're having some sort of bad experience and you still have to send them to school and then to after-school because you have to be at work, well that's hard.

Since your child will be spending several hours at the program each day, try to stay involved in whatever ways you can.

Are there regularly scheduled parent meetings? Many after-school centers have at least one orientation meeting early in the year to explain how the program works, introduce the staff, and answer your questions. If meetings are not scheduled, find out if the director can meet with you. Ask if there are parent committees or events organized by parents. Can you participate if you choose to?

The following sections describe other considerations to keep in mind as you look at after-school programs:

Your Child's Age

Many after-school programs serve children from kindergarten age to twelve years old and a few include programs for teenagers. A program may be excellent for nine- and ten-year-olds but not appropriate for children of five and six. Some programs are terrific for younger children but simply not challenging enough for older kids. Larger programs generally divide children by age, with each group having a particular counselor. In smaller programs, children of various ages may be together. Talk with the director about what the program is like for someone your child's age.

What do five-, six- and seven-year-olds need?

Starting kindergarten and then going to an after-school program is a lot for a five-year-old to manage. It may take time and special tenderness from the staff to help such a young child cope with the afternoon transition. This mother describes her child's adjustment:

Karen went to an after-school program after kindergarten. I talked to her about where she was going to go after school and I took her there and let her look around, let her meet the person that was going to be taking her. But I guess she still didn't have time to think about what it would really be like, because every day, as soon as the older kids would come, she'd get hysterical and cry. The staff people were very responsive but for a long time, when I would pick her up, she'd say she didn't want to go back. I worked it out with the people there and after a while she adjusted. Some parents are worried about bothering the teachers, but they should ask questions and take care of problems for their children's sake.

Children of this age need one specific counselor to be with each afternoon and consistency in the routines they will follow. This is their second transition of the day, and it's important that they be greeted by a warm, nurturing adult they know, who is interested in the kind of day they have had.

Their afternoon should start off with a snack and a chance to settle in with their group and their counselor in a familiar room. It's better if they stay with their own counselor for the afternoon rather than switching to different people for various activities. They should have a chance to play outdoors and have access to many of the same kinds of materials one would find in a preschool or kindergarten classroom—building blocks, dolls, puppets, art materials, books, puzzles, and Lego bricks.

What do eight- and nine-year-olds need?

Children of this age can usually handle more independence. While they should still have a "home base" and a primary counselor, many kids will enjoy having contact with several members of the staff. Some may want to work on projects in groups—for instance, making a mural, writing and putting on a play, cooking a special snack. Others may prefer to play individually or with one or two friends. Children of this age group particularly enjoy games with structure and rules, such as checkers, cards, and hopscotch. They are interested in learning and practicing skills in many different areas. Their specific interests are likely to be defined by what's currently important within their peer group—jumping rope double dutch, playing baseball, whistling, knowing key sports figures or the latest rock stars. Eight- and nine-year-olds like to feel "big" and generally enjoy being given some responsibilities—reading aloud to younger kids, planning special events and parties, writing a newsletter.

What do ten-, eleven- and twelve-year olds need?

Children of this age want increasing independence and can handle some responsibility. If they feel the program is boring or designed for younger kids, they may refuse to go. They should have a great deal to say about what their program will be like. Some kids may be interested in pursuing long-term projects: organizing into sports teams, forming a band, or building something useful—a puppet stage, a clubhouse, or a cage for pets. Older children may want to branch out from the center and get involved with the surrounding community—going to help out on a local farm, regularly visiting a senior citizens' home, or working on a project with the local parks department. They will also probably need periodic breaks in the regular routine: an afternoon at a skating rink or bowling alley, seeing a show, visiting local museums.

What about Homework?

It is important for you and your child to talk about how to handle homework. After-school programs should provide a quiet place where children who wish to do their homework can do so. Some centers make homework part of the planned afternoon activities, while others leave it up to the child.

You may feel strongly that homework should be done in the afternoon, before the child gets too tired or distracted by other things. If this is your approach, it's best to choose a program that will provide that structure. If, on the other hand, you would rather help your child in the evenings or feel it is her decision when to get the work done, choose a more flexible program.

What about Television?

Experts in school-age child care have differing opinions about television, as do parents. Everyone agrees that television should not be used as a mechanical baby-sitter, but there is controversy over whether, if used in specific ways at certain times, TV may have a place in an after-school center. Here are some things to consider: Is the TV a tool to keep kids quiet and occupied? Is it used to watch particular programs, videotapes, or movies that have some relationship to projects the kids are working on? Is television used for special occasions: a movie shown once a month for older kids? *Sesame Street* on rainy days for little kids? If you see a television, ask about its role in the center. Think about your own feelings on the subject. Would you allow your child to watch certain programs at home in the afternoons? If not, is this a decisive point in choosing a center? It's important for you to know the center's philosophy on the subject and then judge whether or not it's compatible with yours.

Making a Decision

At this point in the evaluation process, you have probably narrowed your choice down to only a few options among the centers you've heard about. Talking with other parents now can be extremely helpful in making your decision. If you do not know anyone who uses a particular program, ask the director for the names of a couple of parents who would be willing to speak with you. Ask the parents how they feel about the program in general. If there were problems, were they able to work them out? How are the activities handled? Is the staff reliable and responsive to the children and parents?

No program is perfect. A great deal depends upon what is most important to you and your child. If you have several options, think about whether your child will do best in a larger or smaller program, what kinds of activities she most enjoys, whether you feel comfortable with the program's philosophy, and the staff's qualifications and training. If your child is eight or older, include her in the decision-making process. Discuss the options that the family has and see if she has a particular preference. She may want to go where her friends are going or to a place that offers certain activities she really enjoys.

If you haven't had the benefit of firsthand observation, you may feel like you are making a decision without enough to go on. Make the best choice you can based on the information you have. Then plan to spend some time observing during the first few weeks. It generally takes a week or two for kids and staff to get to know each other and for the schedule to fall into place. After this initial adjustment period, see how your child feels. Remember, if it doesn't work out, you *can* make a change. This topic will be addressed in Chapter 11, "Changing Child Care Arrangements."

Solidifying the Plan

Once you have made your decision, make sure certain things are taken care of before your child starts in the program. Find out the center's policy about illness: Under what circumstances would they call you to pick up your child early? You should be notified if your child is vomiting or running a fever or has any accident involving injury to the head, possible sprains, or broken bones—anything more serious than a minor scrape or bruise.

The center should provide you with a medical form for your doctor to fill out. You will probably also be asked to sign a consent form permitting the staff to take your child to the hospital in an emergency situation. Though this is standard policy, you should make it clear you would expect to be notified immediately if such a situation should arise.

Make sure the center has both parents' work phone numbers and addresses. Provide the names and phone numbers of your doctor and at least two friends or relatives who could be contacted in an emergency if you cannot be reached.

Make very clear who has permission to pick up your child. *The center should never release your child to anyone other than those you have designated unless you notify them directly about a change of plans.* It is not enough to send a verbal message with your child. The center should receive written notification from you, with the name of the person who will be coming and the time of arrival. In an emergency situation, if you need to phone about a change, it is important to speak with your child as well, so she will be sure you want her to leave with the person who is coming in your place.

Coordinating Arrangements Between School and After-school

If the after-school program is located at your child's school, find out how the transition works. If your child is young, will a teacher accompany him to the place where after-school activities take place, or will he be expected to go on his own? If you have a child under the age of eight, request that someone accompany him to the program and check him in.

If the center is off-site and will be providing a pickup service, make sure your child's school is aware that he is going to that particular program. Find out if the school plans to have an adult waiting with the children until the pickup person arrives. If they don't, find out what your child should do if the pickup person doesn't arrive. Make sure that the program will contact the school if someone other than the usual pickup person will be coming on a particular day—and that the school will take responsibility for notifying your child that a different person is expected and that it's all right to go with her. This may sound like a lot to coordinate but it is crucial, since you will want to tell your child never to go with anyone other than the appointed person unless the designated person at his school says it is okay.

Prepare Your Child in Advance

When you have settled the transition issues, make sure you explain very clearly exactly what the child is to do at school dismissal and whom she should turn to for help if there is a problem. This is especially important for younger children, who will undoubtedly feel apprehensive about getting from one place to the next. Go over it carefully, and several times. Tell your child exactly what will happen when school ends—whether it's her teacher who will take her to the right place or an older child. Make sure she understands that you know where the after-school program is and that you will come to get her *there* when it's time. Whether the program is at your child's school or at a center, it's a good idea to find out the names of other children in her class who will be attending the after-school program so the kids can go together.

Talk to young children about the kinds of activities that will take place during the afternoon. While older children who have been involved in the choice of program won't need this kind of explanation, explore any questions they may have. If you don't have the information they want, call the program and try to get it.

Getting Started

If you have a kindergartner or first or second grader, plan to meet him when school ends the first day and accompany him to the after-school program. This way you can reassure your child and yourself that the transition will work the way it's been planned. You can meet his counselor, help him get settled, and observe the afternoon's activities.

If you have an older child, plan to arrive at the center before pickup time the first day or two so you can see how things are going. Find out if the transition between school and after-school went smoothly. If there was any confusion, speak with the director immediately so the problem will be solved. It will be important to your peace of mind to know that the arrangement is reliable. Otherwise you are likely to worry every day about whether your child has gotten safely from one place to the next. Make sure your child always has phone money and your phone number with him, so he can contact you if there is a problem.

Try to Stay Involved

Your child will do best at the center if you are able to establish a good relationship with the staff and show a continuing interest in the program.

■ Make sure to pick up your child on time. It can be a dreary and anxious experience for children and staff to be waiting around after the program has ended.

- Try to arrive early enough to check with your child's counselor about how the afternoon was spent.
- Encourage your child to talk about how things are going, what she's doing, who her friends are, and how she's getting along with her counselor. It's easy to focus on finding out about the day at school, but after-school is an important time for your child as well.
- If problems arise, deal with them promptly. It's difficult to talk in depth at pickup time, so it's best to schedule a time when you can talk to the counselor or director on the phone or meet in person.
- If parent meetings, potluck suppers, holiday parties, or performances by the children are planned, do your best to attend.

As your child gets older, you will probably gradually taper off such arrangements. The problems of teenagers with working parents are beyond the scope of this book, but we couldn't resist the story one woman told about her teenager's ambivalence. On the one hand, the girl certainly did not want child care. She was proud of her mother's career and enjoying her own increasing independence. But one evening, when the subject of clothes came up, the following dialogue took place:

Mother: "I think we should shop for some new blouses for you. Summer's coming."
Daughter: "How could you possibly know what I wear? You leave for work every morning before I get dressed."
Mother: "Because I wash your clothes every week, that's how I know."

Summer Camps

Summer is an exciting time for kids, a chance to break away from the routine of school, have new experiences, and meet new people. But summer child care can be a challenge for parents. First you have to find a camp or other arrangement and then cope with the time "around the edges." Summer programs often don't begin for a week or two after school ends and frequently they end before school starts up again in the fall. It can be difficult to fill in those gaps, and many parents cope by taking their family vacations during these times.

When making summer plans, you may discover that what you have in mind is in conflict with how your child wants to spend her time, as this Minnesota parent noted:

For the first three grades of school, I registered Ellen in summer camp and all these different activities. Then I found out she was going around the neighborhood complaining to the neighbors that her mom wouldn't let her stay home.

The neighbors would report back to me about my poor child, who was over-programmed.

Where you live will have a big impact on what options are available and what children typically do. In some parts of the country, families tend to piece together a variety of plans to cover the long summer vacation—a week or two at a special program run by the parks department, the local YMCA, a visit with grandparents. . . . In other areas, the best option for covering the long summer vacation seems to be camp —either day camp or sleep-away camp. Sending kids away to summer camp for all or a substantial part of the summer is much more common on the East Coast than elsewhere. In fact, the majority of sleep-away camps are in the Northeast, though, of course, there are long-established camps in other parts of the country.

In general, children under eight are probably not ready to go away from home and family for a long period of time. Of course there are exceptions. For instance, a younger child may really want to go to sleep-away camp if an older sibling or good friend is going. And, of course, not all older kids are interested in going away to camp. If your child's good friends are staying around for the summer, she may not want to miss time with them, and there may be excellent local programs that offer the activities she likes.

The following sections will give you information that may help you decide which situation would be best for your family:

Day Camps

The thing about day camp is that you are not only looking for child care, you're also looking for some place where your child can enjoy herself. And a lot of the time you don't know that until the experience is over. I mean, she's been in school for ten months, and what do you do with her?

You should begin gathering information about summer day camps in January. If you have access to a child care resource and referral agency (page 203), the counselors will be able to give you information about summer programs in your area. They can tell you what age groups are served, the kinds of activities available and give you information about fees. You can also ask at your child's school and check with community organizations—YMCAs, girls' and boys' clubs, churches, and synagogues. Many communities have summer programs run by the parks and recreation departments, beach clubs, and other local organizations. As in all child care detective work, other parents are an excellent resource. Find out where your child's friends have gone and give their parents a call.

If your son or daughter has been attending an after-school program that also runs a summer day camp, this is certainly an option to consider. The director and staff and some aspects of the program may be different during the summer, but if you've been happy with the basic philosophy and facilities and your child is amenable, you may want to stick with the program.

YMCAs and other local organizations often hold camp fairs, where representatives from several camps are available to talk with you and your child. This is a terrific way to get information on a number of camps at one time.

In many cases, you will have to make a selection without being able to observe a day camp in operation, so it's important to get as much information as you can. Begin by requesting that the camp staff send you whatever written material they have, but bear in mind that elaborate literature doesn't necessarily mean the camp is good. If what you read sounds really good, follow up with a phone call. Make a list of all your questions beforehand. The director will probably be your best source of information. Many camps hold open houses or orientation meetings in the early spring. At these functions, you can meet the director and some of the key staff members and perhaps see slides of the camp activities.

Here are some basic questions to consider in choosing a day camp:

Activities

What kinds of activities are most important to you and your child? Does she love sports? Would she be happiest spending most of her time doing physical activities like swimming, tennis, or baseball? Does she have a passion for gymnastics? For computers? Would she prefer a program that concentrates on arts and crafts or music? On nature studies? Would a varied program be best for her? One with lots of field trips? There are day camps that fit each of these needs, though they may not all be available in your area.

Location and Hours

Where is the camp located? How far is it from your home? What are the hours? Will your work schedule permit you to drop off your child in the mornings and pick her up in the afternoons? Does the camp provide transportation? How much does it cost? Summer day camps are frequently not geared to the hours of parents who work full-time. Many run from 9:00 A.M. to 4:00 P.M., though they may provide pre-camp supervision in the early morning and post-camp supervision for the late afternoon. There will almost certainly be an additional fee for this service.

Fees

Fees for summer day camps vary tremendously. Those run by municipalities and nonprofit organizations tend to be less expensive than private camps, but few of them are free. Sometimes scholarships are available for eligible families. If you will need to pay for transportation or coverage beyond the camp's regular hours, make sure to include these costs when you figure out the total cost of the camp.

This New York mother faced the economic realities of day camp:

You try to look for programs that are offering some sort of skill-building, but it still goes back to what's affordable. The ones where you are learning some computer skills, or whatever, are very expensive and your average working parent is just not going to be able to afford it.

Transportation

If you live in a city, you may decide on a day camp in the country or at the beach. For city kids, this can be a nice change of scene. Since traveling is involved, it's important to find out how much time your child would be spending on a bus each day. Would he be among the first or the last to be picked up? Would he feel comfortable with the daily trip? What kind of buses are used? Who are the drivers? Are there counselors on board to supervise, or is the driver the only adult? Are there seat belts for each child?

Facilities and Program

Because your child will spend his time relatively far away from you, it's important to inspect the camp site before making a decision. What kind of facilities are provided? Is there an outdoor pool, a lake with a boating and water skiing program? There may be tennis courts and perhaps horseback riding. Are the instructors well trained and experienced? Are children who ride required to wear hard hats? Are field sports, like baseball and soccer, part of the program? What about indoor facilities for rainy days? What kinds of activities other than sports do the children participate in?

If it's a city-based camp, are there good outdoor play areas? What kinds of sports are offered? Are the children taken to an indoor or outdoor pool every day? What other activities are available? Arts and crafts? Drama? Gymnastics? Are the physical surroundings attractive? Kids cooped up in school all year appreciate some trees, birds, and open spaces.

What Is a Good Day Camp Like?

Whatever your family's personal preferences, there are certain features that any good camp should have:

Program Designed for Fun

Summer camp isn't school and shouldn't feel like it. This is a vacation for kids, time to have fun, make new friends, and share experiences that are special to camp life—a camp sing, a scavenger hunt, or a nature hike. It's also a good time to try new things, with the encouragement of supportive adults. Camp is the place where many children learn to swim and dive, play tennis and volleyball, ride a horse—sports they'll enjoy the rest of their lives. Children should be encouraged to have new adventures and take advantage of what's offered, but they shouldn't be pressured to participate in activities they aren't ready for.

Younger children need some consistency in their daily schedule, guidance in choosing activities, and the opportunity for quiet times within an active camp schedule. Older kids should be allowed to make choices about how to spend their time so they can concentrate on their favorite activities. Find out what the daily schedule is like for someone of your child's age. Do younger campers have a quiet rest time after lunch? Do older campers go on more frequent trips?

Pleasant and Safe Environment

Whether city- or country-based, the camp facilities should be well maintained and safe. All equipment should be in good condition. Indoor areas should be bright, cheerful, and well ventilated. Outdoor spaces should be free of litter, glass, and other hazards. Swimming pools, ponds, or lakes should be partitioned into shallow and deeper areas so those children not yet able to swim have a safe place to learn. There should be adequate and clean toilet facilities, well stocked with toilet paper, soap, and paper towels. If meals are provided by the camp, lunches should include fresh fruits and vegetables, protein, carbohydrates, milk, or juice. Food should be ample and attractively served in pleasant surroundings. Nutritious snacks should be available for children who want them in the afternoon. All foods should be refrigerated, and the kitchen area should be clean, with no evidence of bugs or mice.

Qualified and Caring Staff

The camp director is responsible for hiring and supervising the staff. It's important that this person be qualified as well as accessible to parents. Find out whether the camp hires skilled and experienced specialists to supervise various camp activities. You'll want the person who teaches tennis, for example, to know a lot about the game, and if swimming, horseback riding, gymnastics, or other high-risk activities are offered, it's essential to make sure those in charge are fully qualified both to teach and enforce safety precautions. Make sure there are enough people available to watch the children who are participating in these sports. Many camp counselors are college, or in some cases, high school students. You should ask their ages and the criteria for hiring them. Find out how closely they are supervised by the director and whether they receive some sort of training and orientation before the camp season begins.

Camps generally divide children by age, with a specific counselor in charge of each group. For younger children (four to seven), group size shouldn't be more than ten children with one adult. For older children (eight to twelve), one adult with up to fifteen kids is adequate. However, when the kids are involved in sports—ball games, riding, swimming, gymnastics—there should always be additional adult supervision.

Making a Decision

Your decision will depend on what's available in your locality, what you can afford, and what kind of experience you and your child feel would be the most fun. Since you probably won't have seen the camps in operation, it may be difficult to feel sure about a decision. A good camp director will understand this and be patient in answering many questions.

Avoid situations where you feel pressed to make a decision or feel that the staff doesn't want to be bothered with your questions and concerns. A good staff attitude may be crucial in helping you decide:

I was getting worried as summer got closer and we hadn't made plans for my daughter. I saw a brochure about a new day camp being run by a community center. It offered lots of different afternoon activities, but this was the first year they were going to run a summer camp. I figured the first year of anything is usually not very well organized, but when I talked to the director, I was won over. He was patient answering my questions and he invited me to come with Nancy and observe the regular program, see the place, and meet some of the staff. We liked what we saw, but really it was his attitude that reassured me. The way it turned out, my daughter had a great time.

If you know other parents who have used the camp, talk to them. If you don't, ask the director for the names of a few parents you can call. Parents are an excellent source of information. Ask them specific questions about how activities were handled, what they liked most, and how they felt about the director and staff. Find out if they had any problems and, if so, how they were resolved.

A child of seven or older will probably want to be involved in the decision, but if you only have a few options, explain that to him. You may not be able to find the ideal camp, but you can figure out your priorities together.

Getting Ready

The camp should provide you with medical forms for your doctor to fill out. These should be in the camp's files before your child starts, as should both parents' phone numbers and the names and numbers of additional contacts—friends or relatives—who can be reached in an emergency.

It is standard procedure for camps to ask you to fill out a trip permission slip and a release form allowing them to seek hospital attention for your child in an emergency. Make sure they understand that in such a situation you would expect them to contact you immediately. It is important that the camp staff know who will be bringing and picking up your child and that they assure you they will *never release him to any other adult without hearing directly from you that there is a change in plans.*

If your child is old enough to come and go from the camp program by himself, you should inform the staff of this arrangement. If he will be coming and going on camp-provided transportation, make sure you are both clear about the time and place for the morning pickup and the afternoon return. A child who will be waiting for the bus alone in the morning should be given clear instructions on what to do if the bus doesn't show up by a certain time. If your child will be coming and going by himself, make sure he always has phone money, your phone number, and the camp's number with him.

Prepare Your Child for Camp

Make sure your child has whatever you have been told is needed: a lock for her locker, a bathing cap, sneakers. Take her with you when you shop for these items. Tell your child what you know about the facilities and counselors and the kinds of activities available. An older child will be able to read the literature and, if she has participated in the decision, will probably be looking forward to the experience. Younger children who have never been to camp have no idea what to expect. Be as specific as you can about what the schedule will be like and who the counselor will be, and talk about the new friends they will make. If you have a young child going to a local camp, plan to stay for a while with her the  first morning, so you can meet her counselor and help her get settled. Some older kids will want to push you right out the door, feeling embarrassed by having a parent around, but it's still a good idea to arrange your schedule so you can stay if your child wants you to.

Some kids have a difficult time the first week or so. They may not find it easy to settle into a new routine and might be shy about making friends. They may feel anxious if they don't yet know how to swim. Work with the counselor to try to make the transition easier.

Stay Involved

Try to leave a few minutes in the morning and at pickup time to check in with your child's counselor about how things are going. If your child comes and goes in camp-provided transportation, try to arrange to take him or pick him up occasionally so he can show you some of the things he's doing and introduce you to his friends and so that you can touch base with his counselor. If this isn't possible, phone the director to chat about how things are going.

Encourage your child to tell you about his day, the friends he's making, and activities he's participating in. If he is unhappy, try to find out exactly what the problem is, and discuss it promptly with the counselor or director.

If there are events to which parents are invited—visiting day, potluck supper, sports exhibition, or a play—do your best to be there.

Sleep-Away Camps

Sleep-away camp can give both parents and children a little breathing time, an opportunity for adventures and freedom. If you are considering sleep-away camp, your own childhood experiences are likely to play a part in your thinking.

Did you long to go to camp and never make it? Or do you feel you were sent away when you were too young? Was the experience a nightmare you would like to forget or a time you think back on fondly— remembering the friends you made and your feeling of independence. Try to put your memories in perspective so you can make a good judgment about what is best for your child.

For your child to enjoy camp, she must be ready to leave home. Many children feel a little homesick the first few nights at a sleep-away camp and then get over it. But if a child is too young or insecure about leaving you, the experience can be hard.

Expressing an interest in the idea of going away to camp can be a sign that your child is ready. It's not, however, always reliable. She may know other kids who are going and think it sounds like fun without really understanding what the prolonged separation would be like. Think about other times she's been away from home. How did it work out? Has she ever been away for more than a night or two? Would she benefit from time away? Learn to be more independent? Get to know kids outside her own circle?

Many children have their first sleep-away experience at Boy Scout or Girl Scout camps or those run by YMCAs. These camps typically offer one- or two-week options, which can be great for first-time campers.

Choosing a Sleep-Away Camp

Choosing a summer camp is a fairly complicated business that obviously involves a lot of careful research and planning. Consult the American Camping Association for guidance (see page 201), but bear in mind that it is a trade association supported by the camps. The ACA puts out a yearly guide for parents, called *A Guide to Accredited Camps*. This booklet describes the facilities, activities, and costs of all camps accredited by the association.

There are also private-camp advisory services in some localities that will give you information and counseling about which camps may best suit your child's needs. Many of these services are free to parents—the camps pay a fee for each child enrolled. This, of course, means that the service has selected particular camps as clients. This is not necessarily bad, but it does mean you should be cautious in accepting advice without a careful check of your own. Ask any advisory service what arrangements it has with camps. The service may visit all the camps it refers you to. It may ask for comments from campers at the end of each summer.

The most common way to choose a camp is by word-of-mouth. Talk to the parents of your child's friends. Your child also is likely to mention the names of camps that her friends have been to: "Ava goes there and loves it." Relatives and friends with older kids are also a good resource. This may be the most useful and convenient way to find a good camp, but even this method needs good monitoring.

There are so many different kinds of camps that it's a good idea to think about what's important to you and your child before you begin an active search. There are a number of considerations that will help you sort through the camp smorgasbord and select the most suitable:

What type of program would be most appropriate? Many camps offer a variety of activities—water and land sports, nature, arts and crafts, drama, etc. There are also numerous camps specializing in one area or another. If your child has a very strong interest in gymnastics, horseback riding, tennis, computers, music, or baseball, you may want to narrow the focus of your search to the camps that specialize in these particular activities.

Are you interested in a camp that's coed? One that only takes children of one sex? One that has a sister-and-brother arrangement, with separate sites for girls and boys but some joint activities?

Would your child do well in a highly competitive environment, the kind of camp that divides into teams for ongoing events throughout the summer? Do you prefer the noncompetitive approach?

Would your child be most comfortable in a structured camp, where the day's activities are planned in advance and fairly regular? Or would you prefer a program that allows for choices?

Some camps have a strong, stated commitment to bringing together children from different racial, ethnic, and economic backgrounds. This is almost always mentioned in their literature. If no such statement is made, it often means that the group will be pretty homogeneous. Consider which type of environment you want for your child.

Do you think religious observance has no place in a camp program, or do you prefer a camp that holds religious services? Would nondenominational services be all right with you, or would you want your child to be exposed only to your own religion?

How much can you afford to pay for camp? The cost of sleep-away camps varies greatly. Those sponsored by nonprofit groups and religious organizations tend to be much less expensive than private camps. In general, camps with elaborate facilities and specialized activities cost the most. Some private camps charge as much as $4,000 for a full season. If you have more than one child who wants to go to camp, you may be faced with the dilemma this mother describes:

Last year I sent my son to overnight camp and it cost $650 for the two weeks. He told me when he came home that there were six kids in the little tent. And then he told me, "We brushed our teeth three times a day and the food was wonderful and we did this and we did that." And I said, "My God, that's great. That's what I'm paying for." This year he's not going, because I am making a choice. Now I have two kids' summers to worry about and I figure it's much more important that they each have a good experience than just one of them having a good two weeks at overnight camp.

Try to visit the camps you are considering the summer before your child would attend. This will obviously give you a much better idea of what camp life is like than you can get from looking through a brochure. For many parents, however, this may not be possible. You may not know that your child will be ready the following summer, or you may not have the time to visit all the camps you're interested in.

Many camps are willing to send a representative to your home to answer your questions, and some of them arrange a program for parents and children where slides are shown of camp activities and questions are answered. If this is not the case, you may have to rely on the brochure, telephone calls, and talking with other parents. If you do not know anyone who has attended a particular camp, ask for the names of some parents who would be willing to speak with you. It is very common for parents to phone people they don't know for this purpose. You can learn a lot from a parent about whether the camp provided a safe, enjoyable environment, how competent the counselors were, and how the camp dealt with any emergency situations. If the kids are old enough, your child may want to talk to their child as well.

However you go about gathering information, these are the things you should make sure to find out:

Do the children sleep in cabins? Tents? Cottages with electricity?
Where are toilet and shower facilities located?
How long has the camp been in operation? What are the qualifications of the counselors? Junior counselors? How many children is each responsible for? Do the counselors sleep in the cabins with the children?
Where do the children swim—a pool, a lake, the ocean? How many counselors are on duty during swimming periods? Are one or more certified in lifesaving by the Red Cross? Is the water quality monitored for bacteria? Pollution? Is there boating? If so, what are the rules for camper safety? Are the children always accompanied by an adult when they take a boat out? What kinds of tests must the children pass before being allowed to go out in a boat without an adult?
What are the credentials of the staff for teaching particular sports or crafts? This is particularly important for gymnastics and horseback riding. If proper equipment and instruction are not available, these can be high-risk activities for children.
What is the pattern of the average day? Are certain activities required of all campers? Are there choices to be made? How much free

time is there each day? What kind of supervision is provided during these periods?

What are meals like? Ask to see sample menus. Do the meals include protein, carbohydrates, fresh fruits and vegetables? Are special dietary concerns accommodated? What is the camp's policy on sweets? On food packages sent from home? Do all the kids eat at the same time? Is the dining room pleasant? How many counselors supervise? Is service cafeteria-style?

Does the camp have an infirmary? Is there a doctor or nurse on staff, living at the camp, or on call? What is the nearest hospital? If your child is injured or ill, under what circumstances would the camp call you?

Many camps take children from a broad age range. It's important to find out how things work for someone your child's age. Are there earlier and later bedtimes for children of different ages? If your child is a first-time camper, how will the counselors help him get settled? How do they handle homesickness? Under what circumstances would they let your child call you or give you a call themselves? Do older children have more flexibility in choosing their activities? Do they go on overnight camping trips or other special excursions—dances, or athletic meets with other camps? What kind of supervision is provided?

Making a Decision

Consider the information you have gathered and what's most important to you. Your child may want to go to the camp his friends are going to. It's fun to go to camp with a pal and this eases some of the anxiety about making friends. This can be a deciding factor, unless of course you have serious reservations about your child's choice. It's hard to know for sure how a camp experience will turn out, but if you feel that the camp is safe and the staff is qualified and caring, and your child is enthusiastic about going, the odds are in favor of it working out. If it's your child's first time at the camp, you may want to opt for a two-week or one-month session rather than the whole summer.

Helping to Make It a Good Experience

In some cases, if the camp is far from where you live, your child may be going up on a bus, a train, or even a plane. For many kids, this is a good way to begin: By the time they arrive, they have already made some

friends with the kids traveling with them. However, if you haven't ever seen the camp or you think your child might need your support, you may want to take him yourself. Meeting his counselor, knowing where he will sleep, and seeing his potential friends may make it easier for you, as well as him, to handle the separation. Sometimes, it's hard to be sure which will work best, as this mother discovered:

We were excited about taking our daughter to camp for her first sleep-away experience. She had three friends going to the camp and wanted to go. When we arrived, the camp looked wonderful to us, but Cara became immediately hysterical, jumped in the car, locked the door, and announced she was going home. We didn't take her with us, and it was an agonizing and tearful departure for us all. After a week of I-want-to-come-home phone calls, the reports shifted to "Having a great time—I love it here!" Next year, she'll take the bus!

Make sure your child has all the clothing and equipment he will need. Camps generally provide a list of what's recommended. Your child will feel most comfortable if he has the right kind of flashlight and sleeping bag and enough shorts, socks, etc.

Write a letter or postcard and mail it before your child leaves. Having a letter from you when he arrives can ease any initial anxiety. Mail call is usually an important part of a camper's day. Write often—even if your child doesn't. Some camps see to it that kids write each week. Try sending some stamped, self-addressed postcards along, but don't count on this working. Your child may be too busy to write. If you are worried, contact the camp and speak with the director or your child's counselor.

Kids love packages from home with magazines, small games, funny gadgets, or a stuffed animal. If it is allowed, send fruit or goodies that can be shared with bunk mates. This is a nice way of saying you are thinking about your child and her friends.

Almost all camps have particular visiting days set aside in the summer schedule. Regardless of your child's age, it's important to visit. It can be very lonely even for the happiest of campers—or the oldest—to be without parents when everyone else has theirs around. It is worth making every effort to go on the official visiting day. If, for any reason, you know you will not be able to visit on the assigned day, arrange for a favorite relative or friend to go in your place so that your child has someone with him. Talk to the director in advance about whether you could come on a different day, and make sure the child knows the plan.

The Question of Child Abuse

Over the past few years, many parents have been frightened by reports in the press of alleged child abuse occurring at child care facilities. While there is no question that child abuse is a very real problem, there is little evidence that child care settings pose a particular threat. The majority of those who care for young children are responsible, giving people who have been greatly disheartened by the stigma that a few sensationalized stories have placed upon them.

This does not by any means suggest that you, as a parent, should not be cautious and alert to the possibility of such an occurrence. There are several things you can and should do to minimize the chance of your child being mistreated in any way.

Check Any Child Care Situation Thoroughly

The preceding chapters contain guidelines for how to find, assess, and choose quality child care. There are some things, however, that are so important they bear repeating in the context of child abuse.

Checking References

Before you hire an individual who will come to your home, or to whose home your child will go, it is crucial that you check references thoroughly. Even if a person seems pleasant and responsible, it is too risky to hire her unless you can confirm her previous employment history. Anything that hints at the possibility that the caregiver did not act appropriately in another situation should be taken seriously, and you should look elsewhere. Do not try to explain away a past incident or to look for mitigating circumstances. The reason you're checking references is to turn up just this kind of information.

When you talk to other parents, ask specifically whether the caregiver used physical punishment and whether she and the parent had any disagreements about discipline or about any other potentially abusive situations. If a parent seems reluctant to discuss these matters, try to go further. You cannot assume the other parent's attitudes are the same as yours, so be very specific. Ask if the caregiver, with or without the parent's permission, ever slapped or spanked the child. Were threats used to control behavior? Was the parent entirely comfortable with how the caregiver handled the child's physical care—feeding, diapering, toilet training, bathing, dressing?

When you are considering a child care center, ask about the selection process for employees; whether references have been checked; where new people worked before. Find out if there is always more than one adult present in the room with the children. Talk to other parents whose kids are or have been in the program, to find out if there is anything you should be concerned about.

Visiting

Regardless of how good a program sounds, there is no substitute for firsthand observation. When considering a family day care home or child care center, it is essential that you spend time at the site before deciding whether it is a good place for your child. Notice in particular how discipline is handled and whether the children seem at all afraid of any of the adults. How is affection expressed? Do children seem to avoid contact with particular staff members? When you talk with the directors of programs or family day care providers, ask specific questions about discipline and make sure that no type of physical punishment or verbal abuse is ever used.

Spend Time at the Beginning

Do not leave your child in your home alone with a caregiver until you have spent at least a few days together. During this time, if you observe anything in her responses that makes you uneasy, reconsider the arrangement. If things go smoothly and you feel comfortable about leaving your child, come home when you are not expected sometime during the first week or two to see how things are going, or ask your child's grandparent or a friend to do so.

If you choose a family day care home or child care center, plan to spend time at the program during your child's first few days. This added time to observe will give you a fuller picture of the program than was possible to get in your visit. Again, anything that makes you uneasy should also make you reconsider.

When you have found a program that you like and your child is settled in, drop by a few times when you are not expected to make sure that what you have previously observed is really what goes on when parents aren't around. Once you are feeling confident about your arrangement, it is best to stick to your usual schedule so as not to confuse your child. *However, never leave your child in any situation where you are told that there is a policy that prohibits you from having access to your child at any time.*

Ongoing Monitoring

One way to keep track of your child's well-being is to stay involved—maintain an active presence in the child care situation. Spend time with your child and his caregivers when you can, during a free morning or afternoon, for example. Attend parent meetings and conferences. Try to get to know other parents so you can exchange impressions of how things are going.

What Should You Watch Out For?

There is usually a great deal of physical contact between caregivers and young children. This is the way it should be. The thing to watch for is who initiates the contact and in what context. Children should be held, hugged, and cuddled when they need to be. Be wary, however, if you get the feeling that it is the caregiver who needs the physical contact. Are children held, tickled, pinched, or grabbed when they don't want to be? Do they try to squirm away? Are they told to kiss or hug adults hello or goodbye? Do the children seem afraid of any adult, resistant to going with him or her alone out of the classroom? If you do observe any of these things, it doesn't necessarily mean that children are being abused, but if you feel there is something inappropriate about the adult's behavior, you should investigate. Observe more and discuss your concerns with the program's director. If you still feel uneasy, take your child out of the center.

Unfortunately, something may happen even if you have done everything you can think of to ensure that your child is in good hands. If your child tells you that a caregiver hurt or molested her in any way, take it seriously. Small children do not make up stories like these for no reason. Try to find out exactly what your child means. If your child isn't old enough to understand and respond to your specific questions, ask her to show you where she was hurt on her own body or to do it to a doll. If you do suspect abuse, remove your child from the situation until you are convinced that there is another explanation for what she is saying.

There are other, more subtle signs from your child that *may* suggest abuse. However, many events—such as a death in the family, the birth of a sibling, moving, separations from you—can all cause stress in young children. Sometimes just reaching a new stage of development can temporarily make your happy child sad, your outgoing child shy, or your independent child fearful. There can be many causes for the behavioral changes listed below. Because of this, it's important not to panic or jump to immediate conclusions. On the other hand, if you notice any of the following, you should pay close attention and try to determine the cause:

- You see or hear your child saying or doing things in play that seem to be a reenactment of some kind of mistreatment.
- Your child is afraid to go to the child care program or afraid of one particular caregiver and you do not know why.

- Your child begins to act withdrawn, nervous, depressed, develops phobias, or physical symptoms such as headaches or stomachaches.
- Your child is suddenly unusually clingy or fearful of being away from you.
- Your child shows anxiety about using the bathroom, being undressed, or bathing.
- Your child is suddenly frightened of going to sleep at night and/or begins to wet the bed.

In most cases, you will probably be able to figure out the cause for your child's anxieties and be able to give her the support she needs. It is important to be very careful not to make accusations of child abuse unless they are well founded. Such accusations can ruin the reputations and lives of good child care providers. If, however, your exploration of the situation leads you to believe that your child is being mistreated, you should remove her from the situation immediately and get some counseling on how to cope with what's happened.

It is also urgently important that you report your suspicions to your local child welfare agency, to any child abuse hotline, to local child care licensing authorities and to the child care resource and referral agency in your area (see page 203).

11

Changing Child Care Arrangements

*F*inally you've found the care that seems right for your child. The family has made adjustments in its daily life to accommodate the caregiver or center and everything seems to be settled.

And then something happens. You may discover gradually or all at once that there's a problem and you have to deal with an unplanned disruption in your child's care. Perhaps your working hours have changed or the caregiver can no longer work. Perhaps you want a center closer to your home. Or it may be time to move on simply because your child has gotten older and is ready for a different type of setting.

Change will be an inevitable part of your child care experience as your child progresses from infancy through the school-age years. When it occurs, for whatever reason, you will have both practical and emotional issues to handle.

Bringing Closure to a Good Child Care Arrangement

Even the best child care arrangements eventually come to an end. It is certainly a lot easier and less stressful when a change has been planned because you are moving on to something new. However, even if you and your child are looking forward to what's ahead—starting preschool or moving to a new town—saying goodbye is hard. There are a number of ways to bring closure to the experience and help your child make a smooth transition. If the relationship has been good and the change a planned one, the following suggestions may be helpful:

- Talk about the change with your child before it happens, but not too far in advance. Young children don't have the same sense of time adults do. Although it's a good idea to mention the change to a toddler or two-year-old, the information will probably have little meaning until the separation takes place. For three- and four-year-olds, it's best to talk about the change a few weeks before it will occur and then refer to it occasionally as the time approaches. You might want to show your child the days on a calendar and mark the last day. School-age children should feel they're part of any decision to change and should be familiar and, as much as possible, pleased with the arrangement.

- Let the caregiver or teacher know when and how you are explaining the change to your young child, and ask her not to mention it until you have discussed it. Then tell her how your child reacted and ask her to let you know how he seems to be handling the information.

- If possible, plan a special party for the last day. Involve your child in the planning. Pick out favorite foods and decide on decorations and special activities. If your child wants to, let him make a gift for the caregiver or teacher or go shopping with you to pick out something special.

- Take pictures of the caregiver with your child and make sure everyone has a copy to keep. If your child is leaving a family day care home or day care center, take a picture of the whole group, including the provider or teacher.

- Make a specific plan, if possible, to get together sometime soon after the care arrangement ends. If you have an in-home caregiver, invite her to come to your home for a visit after a few weeks have passed. If you are leaving a family day care home or center, try to plan a definite day to return for a visit or at least to get together with your child's special pals. It makes saying goodbye easier when a child knows there is a definite plan to meet again. If you or the caregiver are moving or cannot get together for other reasons, plan a time to talk on the telephone.

- Give your child an opportunity to express his feelings by letting him know how you feel. If the relationship has been good, tell him that you feel sad and will miss the person who has taken such good care of him. Let him know that his caregiver or teacher will continue to think about him and love him even though they won't be seeing each other all the time. If he seems resistant to talking about it, don't push. Children handle their feelings about separation in a variety of ways. Your child may express sadness or anger or act as if nothing has changed. Don't expect any particular reaction. It may even turn out that your child was less attached to the caregiver than you thought and takes the change in stride. Follow his lead: If he asks about the caregiver, respond to his questions; if he wants to contact her, do so. For some children it may be too painful to deal with the separation when it occurs. They may not mention the caregiver for several weeks or even months.

- Be positive about the new arrangements you have made. If your child is starting preschool or kindergarten, talk about what it will be like and the fun he will have there. If you will be having a new caregiver, tell him about the new person, what she is like, and what they will do together.

My little boy seemed to handle the transition from his caregiver to a day care center pretty well. She took care of him part-time the first few weeks during the phasing in at the center. On her last day, we had a little party, and though we hadn't talked about it, we all had gifts for each other. She had gotten my son a lunch box to use for day care. I thought that was perfect! What really took me by surprise was *my* anxiety about the ending. She had taken care of my son for two years and we got very close—shared a lot of ups and downs in our personal lives. I was really grateful to her for all the good care she had given my son and just plain sad that I wouldn't be seeing her every day. We both cried and hugged a lot. We've kept in touch, but we're both busy and our schedules don't match up. Jody talks about her, sometimes saying he misses her —a phone conversation really seems to help.

Dealing with Unanticipated Changes

Be Prepared

Even if the arrangement you have seems to be going well, it is not a bad idea to give some thought to what would happen if you had to make a change. Having a backup plan, even if it's just for a short emergency period, will keep you from rushing into a new situation out of desperation. Discuss with relatives and friends whether they might be able to fill in if necessary. Try to save some vacation days in case you need them. Keep the names and numbers of caregivers, family day care providers, or centers that you liked in your initial search, so if you have to look again you will have a good head start.

The most stressful situation is when your child care arrangement comes to an abrupt and unexpected end, as happened to this mother:

Marian had worked for me for several months and I thought we had a pretty good relationship, but one day she just didn't show up. I was very worried that something had happened to her, but I couldn't reach her. I heard later from someone who knew her that she was okay, but I never found out what happened. If it hadn't have been for helpful family and friends, I would have been in big trouble.

When you depend on in-home or family day care, the person may become ill, take another job, or have a family crisis she must attend to. What can you do? If it's possible, try to buy some time. Even a few days of notice is better than nothing. It will give you a chance to tell your child there will be a change and allow her to say goodbye to the person who has been caring for her. It will also give you at least a little time to set up a temporary arrangement.

Sometimes, something unexpectedly dramatic happens and it is *your* decision to end an arrangement on the spot. You discover your caregiver drunk and asleep when you come home, or your child playing in the yard without supervision when you go to pick her up at the family day care home. In such situations, where your child's safety seems to be at risk, it's best to remove her from the situation immediately and use your backup plan.

Frequently, the realization that you have made a mistake comes more gradually. Perhaps the in-home caregiver who seemed very nice at first has become much too harsh and strict with your child; or the family day care provider has added more children to the group, and your child simply isn't getting the attention he needs. Maybe the wonderful teacher you observed when choosing a day care center resigned over the summer. You aren't comfortable with her replacement and your child is consistently unhappy. Sometimes, problems begin when your child reaches a new stage of development, as this East Coast mother describes:

I went back to work when my son was three months old. I put an ad in the paper and I found a woman who was very good with him when he was an infant. She loved to hold him and interact with him and everything seemed to be going along well until he started walking and toddling, at about eleven months. Then we started to have real problems. She was not licensed, they had no insurance, and her husband was really worried that something was going to happen. I would come in the door at the end of the day and Sam learned to jump out of the playpen and run. You know, he was just so excited to see me. One day, when I turned to talk to her, he started to go out the door. They told me that I was a horrible parent because I didn't know how to control him, and we had a huge fight. I decided if this was their opinion of me—and I thought I was doing pretty well, all things considered—that I needed to find other caregivers.

Even when you are very dissatisfied and sure of your decision, it can be awkward to tell the person who cares for your child that you want to end the arrangement. If that person has been living in your home, it can be even harder.

This parent describes what that was like:

The problem with in-home care, at least that I find, is that you take on a responsibility for the person too. It's not easy, when things go wrong, to say to someone who is in your home, "Okay, thanks very much, it's time for you to go."

You will have to decide how to handle the dismissal in a way that is comfortable for you and that does not cause an unnecessarily stressful situation. If you want to specify your reasons, do so; if not, simply say that there has been a change in your situation and you will no longer need the care. It is best, if you can manage it, not to have this conversation in the presence of your child, so you can explain it to her in your own way at an appropriate time. If you have a contract, it may contain a provision for termination notice and payment. If you are comfortable using the care for a few more weeks, you can use that time to look for an alternative arrangement. But if your child has been put at risk or you feel the caregiver may treat her punitively as a result of your decision, it's better to end the arrangement immediately.

Whether or not it was your decision, the unanticipated end of a child care arrangement can make you feel as if the bottom has dropped out of your carefully organized life. You have to deal with the immediate practical problems as well as with your child's feelings and your own. It's a stressful time. Try to take things one step at a time.

Use your backup system. A family member or friend is the best choice at this time. If the situation has been traumatic, it will be the most reassuring if you or your spouse can take a few days off to stay with your child.

If you have access to a child care resource and referral agency (page 203), contact it for help. The counselors will give you the sympathy you no doubt crave. They will help you think through your best alternatives for both a short-term and long-term arrangement and give you referrals for care in your community.

Your child will need your help through this experience. Exactly what you say and do will, of course, depend partly on his age, the reason for the change, and how long your child was with the caregiver. Whatever the circumstances, it's important to take some time to sort out your own feelings. You may feel angry and betrayed. Talk about it first with a friend or your spouse, so you can separate your emotions from what your child may be feeling. If he was very attached to the caregiver, her sudden departure from his life will be very confusing. A beloved caregiver is, after all, a substitute parent. Even with a very young child, it's good to give a simple and honest explanation of what happened, but bear in mind that your explanation may not really be understood. All your child knows is that she was there one day and is gone the next. Such an experience is likely to raise anxiety that you, too, might disappear, so you need to reassure him with actions as well as words. Try to spend as much time with your child as you can and make sure that when you leave him, you come back exactly when you said you would. Your child may be able to verbalize some of his feelings, or you may have to interpret some subtle messages—regressive behavior, increased anxiety, temper tantrums that seem to have no cause. A great deal of physical and verbal reassurance may be necessary, but if you give him consistent love and support, the child will most likely find a way to express his feelings and be able to accept your comfort.

If the caregiver was in some way abusive or neglectful, a child will probably be relieved to see her go. Make sure to tell him that what happened was not his fault and that you will keep him safe. He will probably need a lot of help and reassurance in dealing with what may have been an unpleasant relationship, and he may be fearful of what comes next. Take time in making a new arrangement. It is very easy when you are under pressure to make hasty decisions. Try to avoid grabbing the first alternative that presents itself, unless it is a good one. If at all possible, stick with your temporary arrangement until you find a new child care situation that you feel reasonably sure will work out well for the long term. Plan to spend time helping your child adjust to the new arrangement, so you can reassure him and yourself that this experience will be a happy one.

What If You Are Not Sure Whether to Make a Change?

Sometimes it just isn't clear whether you should make a change. You may feel dissatisfied with some aspects of the situation but not sure you can do better. The care that your child is receiving may be adequate but not really *good*. Perhaps the person working in your home is keeping your child safe and comfortable but not playing with her enough or taking her anywhere. Or the family day care provider is offering only a limited choice of activities and you think your child isn't getting the stimulation she needs. The teacher in your child's day care classroom seems to spend all her time handling a few disruptive kids and doesn't seem very aware of who your child is and how she's spending her time.

In cases like these, it's generally a good idea to see if you can improve the situation before deciding to make a change. Try to think specifically about the problem areas, and plan a time when you can talk with the caregiver or teacher. It may just be a question of expressing your concerns and letting the caregiver or family day care provider know exactly what you feel is lacking.

This mother was able to resolve a problem by talking it through:

The woman where I took my child every day was worried about her own children and how they were doing with these other kids around. Her son was hitting and it was: "I can't take responsibility, he's going to hurt your daughter and

I'm not . . ." and I said, "Wait, let's slow down, let's look at the situation." And we sort of talked through it and we really did solve the problem about both how her child was reacting to mine and how mine was reacting to hers.

If your child is in a center, you may choose to talk with the director rather than the teacher. Often, such discussions can be very productive and can result in tangible changes. The director may be able to give the teacher some assistance in how to better manage the group, and help facilitate a meeting where you can talk to the teacher directly about what's troubling you. It may also be helpful to talk with some other parents and see how they feel. If you are not alone in your criticisms, you can suggest a group meeting to discuss your concerns.

You can't always fix things. The caregiver or teacher may see the situation differently than you do and you may remain unsatisfied. Before you decide on a change, however, consider the following:

- How is your child doing? What does she say about her caregiver or teacher? Is she unhappy? Perhaps the things that are bothering you do not have the same impact on your child. If she is happy and safe, it may be best to maintain the status quo. Consistency is important to a young child and should be a factor in your decision.
- Are there better options available? Visiting some other programs and talking with friends about their child care can give you some perspective on the situation. You may find something closer to your ideal or you may feel after looking around that the problems you are dealing with are relatively minor.
- Think about ways you could supplement the care arrangement to make it better. For instance, if you feel your child isn't getting enough stimulation with an in-home caregiver or family day care provider, perhaps you can arrange to have him go to a morning play group a few days a week. Or if your child is spending the whole day at a day care center, perhaps you could find someone to pick him up earlier and take care of him in your home for the rest of the day.

In such situations, you need to weigh the pros and cons and decide in what areas compromise is acceptable. If you ultimately feel that a change is best, following the applicable guidelines in the first section of this chapter may make the transition easier.

Advocating for Our Children

*I*n this book we've been describing what you should look for in child care, what the best situations should be like—the ones you and your children deserve. This kind of excellent care is available and we hope you've found it easily. But the truth is that if you have, you're one of the relatively few lucky ones.

For most of us, finding good child care is a major challenge. We are often shocked by the poor quality of what we see and frustrated by the high costs. Of course each family has its own particular needs and desires, but millions of working parents in this country stumble over the very same obstacles in the child care maze. And just as these are not individual problems, the solutions are neither simple nor individual.

Why is the situation so bad? What are the specific problems? How can they be overcome?

In the first place, the problem is enormous. if you had a hard time finding good care, it's because you were fighting against the odds. The demand for child care is much greater than what is available. Since the 1970s the number of children under age six whose mothers work outside the home has increased by 80 percent. With current trends expected to continue, by 1995 nearly two thirds of children under six (15 million), and over three fourths of all school-aged children (28 million) will have mothers in the labor force. On the supply side, there are currently only an estimated 2.5 million spaces for children under six in licensed child care centers and family day care homes.

The crisis for our very youngest children is acute. The lack of a national policy on parental leave means that the vast majority of parents must risk losing their jobs if they wish to remain at home for an appropriate time after the birth of a child. Mothers return to work before they are physically or emotionally ready and often must leave their babies in inadequate care situations. In 1990 both houses of Congress passed a modest parental leave bill only to have it vetoed by the president.

Although there are hundreds of thousands of individuals and organizations caring for children, there is little logic as to where services are, when they are open and how they function. Parents have difficulty finding care that matches the hours they work. This is particularly true for people who work on evening and weekend shifts in factories and hospitals, as well as in police and fire departments. The work these parents do is vital to society, but they are given little help in coping with their child care problems. In some areas there are open spaces in child care centers and family day care homes. In most places, however, parents are met with long waiting lists and few desirable options. Tens of thousands of families in the work force need care for infants and toddlers and school-age children, yet the majority of center care is designed for children between the ages of three and five.

While care is difficult to find for all children, the current system has virtually ignored families who have children with special needs. There are few facilities equipped, either physically or in terms of trained staff, to provide the type of specialized care that is required.

Yet these issues are still only part of the child care challenge. There is more at stake for our children than the practical questions of setting up a system that allows parents to hold down jobs outside the home. How our children spend the hours they are away from us is of paramount importance. Their *care* and *early education* are one and the same. We now know that quality care must include appropriate learning experiences from infancy through the school-age years. It makes a significant difference in how well children develop—how they get along with others, how well they do in school and in their later lives. All children deserve a good start in life, whether their parents are working, in job training, or in school. Care is not enough. Adequate care is not enough. Our children deserve the highest quality care and education that we can provide.

Government regulations *should* be the first step in ensuring high quality care and education, but they vary tremendously from state to state. Even where there are good regulations, they are frequently not effectively enforced nor do they cover all child care situations. Many thousands of people have provided and continue to provide care outside of any regulated system. Some of this care is excellent, but the laxity of appropriate regulations has also made it possible for virtually anyone who wishes to care for children to do so. There are far too many child care services across the country that have unskilled staffs, take too many children and operate in unsafe facilities. Thousands of families must accept this very substandard care because they have no choice.

The keys to quality are not hard to find. Years of research have clearly defined what is needed. We know what makes for a safe environment for children. We also know what kind of training and skills the people who care for them should have, and the best adult/child ratios for each situation. Thus far, such expert advice has frequently been ignored. Quality care is costly, and the public and private sectors of our economy have been slow to make the financial investment that is required.

Most parents can't afford excellent child care. They are often forced to make decisions based on cost rather than quality or else they must make great sacrifices in other areas.

This is only one piece of the financial puzzle. We know that the quality of care our children receive is directly dependent on the training and skills of the people who provide that care. Yet caregivers and teachers get little respect or acknowledgment for the important work they do, and they certainly don't earn adequate wages. Good financial compensation is not one of the rewards of working with young children, and yet, from the point of view of what our families and our country need, it certainly should be.

Training is not easily accessible or affordable to those in the child care field. Despite the recent development of a handful of "nanny schools," most women who work as in-home caregivers cannot afford the time or money for such programs. Family day care providers have the demanding job of caring for small groups of young children, yet there are few training opportunities for them, and in many states, no particular credentials are required for this important work.

And just at a time when the need for good child care is so pressing, many of the most qualified people are leaving the field. Teachers with master's degrees in early childhood education typically earn less than entry-level clerical workers. Many people who work in the child care field lack even such basic benefits as health insurance, paid vacations and sick leave. The fact that teacher training programs are having a hard time recruiting students seems perfectly understandable.

Young adults who are excited about working with children often teach for a few years and then, when they start their own families, must look for jobs with higher salaries. According to a recent study by the Child Care Employee Project, directors of child care centers reported a 41 percent turnover rate annually for their teaching staffs. Not surprisingly the most important predictor of turnover is salaries—the centers that experience the highest turnover rate pay the lowest salaries.

Given the range of problems, is it any wonder most parents have a hard time finding good child care? But defining problems can be a useless exercise unless it leads to solutions. We know what's wrong. How do we fix it? How do we ensure that regardless of their incomes or where they live, good affordable child care is available to every family that needs it?

We believe that a good child care system must include the following:

- **An adequate supply of the full range of child care services from infancy through the school-age years.**   Such a system should offer options that meet the diverse needs and preferences of the families who use it. Services should be available in a variety of settings including family day care homes, day care centers, nursery schools, community centers, Head Start programs and the public schools. Planning must include facilities designed to accommodate children with special needs.
- **National minimum standards for child care centers and family day care providers.**   These should reflect what we know about quality care, based on the research and advice of experts. While communities should certainly be encouraged to set the highest possible local stan-

dards, national guidelines would serve as a safeguard to ensure that there are at least minimum standards. Once in place, these regulations must be enforced. The agencies responsible must have enough skilled workers to do the job well. Every effort should be made to encourage centers and family day care providers to obtain the appropriate licenses. They should be offered the incentives of training, technical assistance, higher wages and benefits.

- **A skilled pool of caregivers and teachers.** Training has a direct impact on improving the quality of care. Courses in child development, nutrition and first aid should be easily accessible and affordable to in-home caregivers, family day care providers and those who work in child care centers. Grants and scholarships should be available to those who wish to pursue careers as teachers in early childhood education. Salaries should reflect the difficult and demanding nature of the job. As teachers acquire more training and experience, they should receive greater financial compensation. All child care workers should be assured of the basic benefits that most other jobs offer.

- **Adequate mechanisms to insure that care is affordable.** Family income cannot be the determining factor by which children receive quality care. Care and early education should be free to those who cannot afford to pay for it. Subsidies and sliding scale fees should be available to assure parental access to a full range of child care choices. This funding should be adequate to cover all families who need assistance.

- **A nationwide network of resource and referral agencies.** For a diverse system to work, parents will need assistance in locating and selecting the best type of care for their children. Resource and referral agencies can provide this service. Because they are community-based, they are in a key position to assess child care needs in their own area and to feed this information to policymakers and planners. Such agencies can also increase the pool of care by recruiting and training family day care providers and in-home caregivers. They can provide technical assistance to individuals, groups and corporations who wish to open child care centers.

Do such ideas seem like pie in the sky? They shouldn't. Many other countries have such systems in place. In France, for example, all child care is regulated, standards are high and costs are kept down. Care for children up to the age of three ranges from $195.00 a year to a maximum of $4,700, based on family income. Preschool care for children between the ages of three and five is free and 98 percent of the children in this age group are enrolled. Care is available for children of all ages from early in the morning to late afternoon. Preschool teachers in France hold the equivalent of a master's degree in early childhood and elementary education. As an incentive to bring qualified people into the child care field, students of preschool education pay no college tuition and receive a stipend in return for promising to work in the field for at least five years following graduation. Family day care is licensed and providers are covered by social security and disability and unemployment insurance, in addition to financial compensation for the job. When the president of France stated, "France will blossom in its children," he seemed to be expressing an attitude that is reflected in the nation's child care policies (*New York Times*, August 1, 1990).

We must make a similar commitment to providing the very best for our children. The features we've been describing cost money. But aren't our children worth it? Shouldn't they take priority in our national budget? The private sector, too, must make a financial commitment. What could be a more important investment?

How such public and private funding is utilized will vary in different communities, and it is on the community level that an appropriate assessment of needs can take place. Funding is needed for training, developing new services and expanding existing programs, as well as bringing the cost of child care down to affordable levels.

How do we get there from here? We should insist that our leaders take a realistic look at the problems and begin to implement solutions. We have made a start. Child care is now moving higher on the agendas of many of our local and national politicians. Legislation is being presented and debated at all levels of government.

Gradually, employers are becoming aware that the child care problems faced by their employees are a contributing factor to high rates of absenteeism and turnover. More than 5,400 employers now provide some form of child care assistance to their employees. While some companies have set up on-site child care centers, this approach to the problem is not yet widespread. Many companies are trying to assist working parents by doing one or more of the following: purchasing enhanced referral services for their employees; providing seminars on child care and other family issues; helping parents to pay for child care; creating more flexible time and leave policies; and providing emergency and sick child care services for their employees.

Religious institutions as well as other organizations involved with families and children have a long history of providing direct child care services. Now they, too, are beginning to become more involved in the broader policy issues.

There have been gains, but we are still a long way from reaching the goal of a good child care system.

What Can You Do?

Parents should speak up about the realities of family life in the 1990s. You know what quality care should be like and what changes must occur to make such care a reality. Your own search for child care has given you an education (and we hope this book has helped).

Now, armed with this information, you can help to educate others. There are a number of roles you can play as parent, community member, and voter:

- When you act as an advocate for your own child, you are taking an important step toward improving conditions for yourself and others. Try to ensure that at least in your own arrangement, care is of the highest quality and the caregivers or teachers are being treated fairly. It is important to encourage and support the efforts of those caring for your children and let them know that they are valued. Make suggestions to your caregiver or family day care provider. Get on the board of your child care center or form a parent committee. If you have complaints, speak up. If you come across bad and unsafe conditions for children, report them to the local authorities.
- Raise your concerns about child care with your friends, in your church, synagogue, community center, PTA—any place where there is an opportunity to speak with groups of parents.
- If you have access to a child care resource and referral agency, ask for information about current legislative issues and about advocacy activities that are being planned by parents and child care workers in your community. If there is no such group where you live, contact

NACCRRA (page 248) to find out how you might help to get such an agency started.

- Bring your child care concerns to the workplace. Many parents are still hesitant to let their supervisors know they are having child care problems. They fear that it may reflect badly on them and possibly hamper them in advancing on the job. Such silence, however, allows some employers to continue to believe that there is no problem. Bear in mind that the issues you are facing are shared by others. Speak with your co-workers so you can address your employer as a group. If you are in a union, make sure the topic becomes a priority issue.

- Remember you are a voter as well as a parent. Contact the politicians who represent you both locally and nationally. If they are uninformed, educate them. Let them know that their stand on child care and family issues will be a crucial factor in how you decide to vote. Testifying at public hearings on child care legislation can be a very effective action, particularly if large groups of parents are involved.

How quickly changes will come about has a great deal to do with people like you. The harder we all push, the faster we will see results. We owe it to ourselves, and we certainly owe it to our children.

Appendix 1

Resources

American Camping Association
Bradford Woods
5000 State Road 67 North
Martinsville, IN 46151-7902
317-342-8456

American Council of Nanny Schools
Delta College
University Center, MI 48710
517-686-9417

National Association for Family Day Care
(NAFDC)
725 Fifteenth Street, N.W. Suite 505
Washington, DC 20005
202-347-3356
1-800-359-3817

National Association for the Education of
Young Children (NAEYC)
1834 Connecticut Avenue, N.W.
Washington, DC 20009-5786
202-232-8777
1-800-424-2460

Project Home Safe
1555 King Street
Alexandria, VA 22314
703-706-4600

Appendix 2

National Au Pair Placement Agencies

The following are eight agencies that the federal government has authorized to bring au pairs into the United States:

Au Pair in America
102 Greenwich Ave.
Greenwich, CT 06830
1-800-727-2437

AuPair/Homestay USA
1015 15 St. NW, Suite 7521
Washington, DC 20005
202-628-7134

EF AuPair
1 Memorial Drive
Cambridge, MA 02142
1-800-333-6056

Au Pair Programme USA
36 S. State, Suite 3000
Salt Lake City, UT 84111
801-943-7788

Au Pair Intercultural
Flavia Hall
Marylhurst College Campus
P.O. Box 147
Marylhurst, OR 97036
503-635-3702
*This program places au pairs in Western
cities only.*

Au Pair Care
1 Post Street Suite 700
San Francisco, CA 94104
1-800-288-7786

EurAuPair
228 North Pacific Coast Hwy.
Laguna Beach, CA 92651
1-800-333-3804

InterExchange
356 W. 34th St.
New York, NY 10001
212-947-9533

Appendix 3

National Association of Child Care Resource and Referral Agencies—Member Agencies

These directories should help you in finding your local child care resource and referral agency. First check the individual agency list to see if a local referral agency is listed. If none is listed, contact the appropriate state organization for the name of the closest referral agency.

STATE	AGENCY	AREA SERVED
Alabama	Child Care Options 457 Conti Street Mobile 35502 205-433-1312	Mobile, Baldwin, Washington counties in Alabama, and Harrison, Hancock, and Jackson in Mississippi
	Child Care Resource Center, Inc. P.O. Box 348 Auburn 36831-0348 205-749-0426	Lee County
	Childcare Resources 309 23rd St. N. Birmingham 35203 205-252-1991	Jefferson, Shelby, Walker, and Blount counties
	Coosa Valley Child Care Resource and Referral Agency P.O. Drawer 1 Talladega 35150 205-362-3852	Talladega, Clay, Randolph, and Coosa counties

STATE	AGENCY	AREA SERVED
Alabama (*cont.*)	Family Guidance Center of Montgomery, Inc. 925 Forest Avenue Montgomery 36106 205-262-6660	Montgomery, Autauga, and Elmore counties in Alabama
Alaska	Child Care Connection P.O. Box 103394 Anchorage 99510 907-278-2273	Municipality of Anchorage
Arizona	Association for Supportive Child Care 2510 S. Rural Road, Suite J Tempe 85282 602-829-0500	Greater metropolitan Phoenix area
	Family Service Agency 1530 E. Flower Phoenix 85014 602-264-9891	Metropolitan Phoenix area
	Tucson Association for Child Care, Inc. 1030 N. Alvernon Way Tucson 85711 602-881-8940	Pima County
Arkansas	Arkansas Child Care Resource and Referral Center 5 Statehouse Plaza Little Rock 72201 501-375-3690	State of Arkansas
California	Bananas, Inc. 6501 Telegraph Ave. Oakland 94609 415-658-0381	Northern Alameda County

STATE	AGENCY	AREA SERVED
California (*cont.*)	CDI—Choices for Children P.O. Box 18295 South Lake Tahoe 95706 916-541-5848	El Dorado and Alpine counties
	Child and Family Services 2406 Kent Street Los Angeles 90038 213-413-0777	Downtown Los Angeles west through Beverly Hills, Hollywood Hills on the north side and Santa Monica Freeway on south
	Child Action, Inc. 2103 Stockton Blvd, #8 Sacramento 95817 916 453 0713	Sacramento and Yolo counties except for the City of Davis
	Child Care Connection 8314 Ruthburn Avenue Northridge 91325 818-349-1815	San Fernando Valley and parts of Ventura County
	Child Care Coordinating Council of San Mateo County, Inc. 1838 El Camino Real, #214 Burlingame 94010 415-692-6645	San Mateo County
	Child Care Resource Center 5077 Lankershim Blvd, #600 North Hollywood 91601 818-762-0905	San Fernando Valley, Burbank, Glendale, Santa Clarita Valley, Antelope Valley
	Child Development Resource Center 809 H Bay Avenue Capitola 95010 408-476-8585	Santa Cruz County

STATE	AGENCY	AREA SERVED
California (*cont.*)	Children's Council of San Francisco 1435 Market Street San Francisco 94103 415-864-1234	San Francisco County
	Children's Services Network of Merced County, Inc. 1701 "N" Street Merced 95340 209-722-3804	Merced County
	City of Davis Child Care Services 23 Russell Blvd Davis 95616 916-756-3747	City of Davis and Davis Joint Unified School District
	Community Child Care Council of Sonoma County, Inc. 2227 Capricorn Way, #105 Santa Rosa 95407 707-544-3084	Sonoma County with the exception of the Russian River area
	Community Connection for Child Care 420 8th Street Bakersfield 93301 805-322-7633	Kern, Inyo, and Mono counties
	Community Coordinated Child Development Council/Santa Clara County 160 E. Virginia #200 San Jose 95112-5888 408-998-4900	Santa Clara County
	Community Resources for Children 1754 Second Street, Suite A Napa 94559 707-253-0366	Napa County

STATE	AGENCY	AREA SERVED
California (*cont.*)	Connections for Children 612 Colorado Avenue #104 Santa Monica 90401 213-452-3202	North Topanga areas to Redondo Beach and the area west of La Cienga
	Contra Costa Child Care 3020 Grant Street Concord 94520 415-676-kids	Contra Costa County
	Crystal Stairs, Inc. 5105 W. Goldleaf Circle #200 Los Angeles 90056 213-299-0199	S. Central Los Angeles, Inglewood, Hawthorne, Lawndale, Gardena
	Family Resource and Referral Center 1149 N. El Dorado Suite C Stockton 95202 209-948-1553	San Joaquin County
	Growth and Opportunity, Inc. 321 San Felipe Road #14 Hollister 95023 408-637-9205	San Benito County
	Human Response Network P.O. Box 2370 Weaverville 96093 916-623-kids	Trinity County
	Humboldt Child Care Council 805 7th Street Eureka 95501 707-444-8293	Humboldt County

STATE	AGENCY	AREA SERVED
California (*cont.*)	Infant/Child Enrichment Services 14326 Tuolumne Road Sonora 95370 209-533-0377	Tuolumne County
	Marin Child Care Council 828 Mission Avenue San Rafael 94901 415-454-7951	Marin County
	Mountain Family Service P.O. Box 919 San Andreas 95249 209-754-1075	Amador and Calaveras counties
	Options 3505 N. Hart Avenue #230 Rosemead 91770 818-280-0777	Lower half of San Gabriel Valley, including Whittier and Lamirada in Los Angeles County
	Plumas Rural Services Child Care Resource and Referral P.O. Box 1079 Quincy 95971 916-283-4453	Plumas County
	Resources for Family Development 1520 Catalina Court Livermore 94550 415-455-5111	Livermore, Pleasanton, and Dublin counties
	River Child Care, Inc. P.O. Box 1060 Guerneville 95446 707-887-1809	Northwestern Sonoma County

STATE	AGENCY	AREA SERVED
California (*cont.*)	Sierra Nevada Community Services Council 256 Buena Vista, Suite 210 Grass Valley 95945 916-272-8866	Nevada and Sierra counties
	Solano Family and Children's Services 2750 N. Texas Street #450-G Fairfield 94533 707-422-2881	Solano County
	Valley Oak Children's Services 1024 Esplanade Chico 95926 916-895-3572	Butte and Glenn counties
	YMCA Childcare Resource Services 1033 Cudahy Place San Diego 92110 619-275-4800	San Diego County
Colorado	Boulder Children's Services P.O. Box 791 Boulder 80306 303-441-3180	Boulder County
	Child Care Clearinghouse 1129 Colorado Avenue Grand Junction 81501 303-241-0190	Mesa County. Towns and suburbs of Grand Junction, Clifton, Palisade, and Fruita. Also, Rangely, in Rio Blanco County
	Family First Resource and Referral—Red Rocks Community College 13300 W 6th Ave. Box 22 Lakewood 80401-5398 303-969-9500	Jefferson County (also have database to cover all of the Denver metro area)

STATE	AGENCY	AREA SERVED
Colorado (*cont.*)	Mile High United Way Child Care Resource and Referral 2505 18th St. Denver 80211-3907 303-433-8900	Adams, Arapahoe, Denver, Douglas, and Jefferson counties
	The Women's Center 424 Pine Street #104 Ft. Collins 80524 303-484-1902	Larimer County
Connecticut	Child Care Connections of Western Connecticut 70 North Street Danbury 06810 203-794-1180	Bethel, Bridgewater, Brookfield, Danbury, New Fairfield, New Milford, Newton, Redding, Ridgefield, Sherman
	North Central Child Care Info Line—Region 4 900 Asylum Avenue Hartford 06105 203-482-9471	North central part of state
	Northeast Child Care Info Line—Region 6 948 Main Street Willimantic 06226 203-456-8886	Northeast part of state
	Northwest Child Care Info Line—Region 5 232 North Elm Street Waterbury 06702 203-482-9471	Northwestern part of state
	South Central Child Care Info Line—Region 2 One State Street New Haven 06511 203-624-4143	South central part of state

STATE	AGENCY	AREA SERVED
Connecticut (*cont.*)	Southeast Child Care Info Line—Region 3 74 West Main Street Norwich 06360 203-346-6691	Southeastern part of state
	Southwest Child Care Info Line—Region 1 83 East Avenue, Room #107 Norwalk 06851 203-333-7555	Southwestern part of state
Delaware	Child Care Connection 3411 Silverside Rd, Baynard #100 Wilmington 19810 302 479 1660	State of Delaware
District of Columbia	Washington Child Development Council 2121 Decatur Place NW Washington 20008 202-387-0002	District of Columbia
Florida	Alachua Community Coordinated Child Care P.O. Box 12334 Gainesville 32604 904-373-8426	Alachua, Levy, Gilchrist, Bradford, and Dixie counties
	Child Care Association of Brevard County, Inc. 18 Harrison Street Cocoa 32922 407-636-4634	Brevard County
	Child Care Central 421 West Church Street Jacksonville 32202 904-630-3698	Duval County

STATE	AGENCY	AREA SERVED
Florida (*cont.*)	Child Care Connection 366 Goodlette Road South Naples 33940 813-649-4816	Collier County
	Child Care Connection of Broward County 4740 N. St. Rd 7 Bld C, #200 Ft. Lauderdale 33319 305-486-3900	Broward County, including Ft. Lauderdale, Pompano Beach, and Hollywood
	Child Care of Southwest Florida, Inc. 1750 17th St., Unit B-2 Sarasota 34234 813-366-2149	Sarasota County (cities of Sarasota, Venice, Nokomis)
	Child Care of Southwest Florida, Inc. 3625 Fowler Street Ft. Myers 33901 813-278-4114	Lee, Hendry, and Glades counties (cities of Ft. Myers, Cape Coral, Sanibel Island, Clewiston, Moore, Haven, Labelle)
	Child Care Options/Latchkey Services 1715 East Bay Drive, Suite H Largo 34698 813-584-7462	Pinellas, Pasco, Manatee, and Hillsborough counties
	Child Care Resource and Referral, Inc. 551 SE 8th St., #500 Delray Beach 33483 407-832-0844	Palm Beach, Martin, St. Lucie, Indian River, and Ocheechobee counties
	Childhood Development Services, Inc. 3230 SE Maricamp Road Ocala 32671 1-800-635-5437	Marion, Lake, Citrus, Sumter, and Hernando counties

STATE	AGENCY	AREA SERVED
Florida (*cont.*)	Community Coordinated Child Care for Central Florida, Inc. 1612 E. Colonial Drive Orlando 32803 407-894-8393	Orange, Osceola, and Seminole counties
	Coordinated Child Care of Pinellas, Inc. 4140 49th St. N. St. Petersburg 33709 813-521-1853	Pinellas County
	Early Childhood Services, Inc. 1241 N. East Avenue Panama City 32401 904-785-0988	Bay, Washington, Holmes, Gulf, Jackson, Franklin, Calhoun, Leon, Wakula, Jefferson, Taylor, Madison, Libery, and Gadsden counties
	Suwannee Valley Community Coordinated Child Care P.O. Box 2637 Lake City 32056 1-800-542-5456	Hamilton, Suwannee, Columbia, Lafayette, and Union counties
	United Child Care, Inc. 801 South Yonge Street Ormond Beach 32174 904-673-3730	Volusia, Flagler, and St. Johns counties
	West Florida Child Care and Education Services, Inc. P.O. Box 12242 Pensacola 32581-2242 904-438-7422	Escambia and Santa Rosa counties

STATE	AGENCY	AREA SERVED
Florida (*cont.*)	YMCA Child Care Resource and Referral 4326 El Prado, #10 Tampa 33629 813-831-5515	Hillsborough, Pasco, and Manatee counties
Georgia	Care Connection 850 College Station Rd, #332 Athens 30610 404-353-1313	Ten-county area of northeast Georgia
	Care Solutions, Inc. 5 Concourse Parkway, Suite #810 Atlanta 30328 404-393-7366	Greater Atlanta area
	Child Care Solutions of North Georgia Gainesville College Gainesville 30503 404-535-6383	Ten-county area: Hall, Banks, Jackson, Barrow, Stephens, White, Lumpkin, Habersham, Dawson, and Forsyth
	Save the Children/Child Care Solutions 1340 Spring St. NW, Suite #200 Atlanta 30309 404-885-1585	Eleven metropolitan Atlanta counties
Hawaii	Parents Attentive To Children (PATCH) 810 N. Vineyard Boulevard Honolulu 96717 808-842-3874	State of Hawaii
Idaho	Child Care Choices, Inc. 1000 West Garden Coeur D'alene 83814 208-765-6296	Kootenai County

STATE	AGENCY	AREA SERVED
Idaho (*cont.*)	Child Care Connections P.O. Box 6756 Boise 83707 208-343-kids	Ada County
	Human Services Center, Inc. 3100 Rollandet Idaho Falls 83403 208-525-7281	Custer, Butte, Clark, Fremont, Jefferson, Madison, Teton and Bonneville counties
	Southeast Idaho Community Action Agency P.O. Box 940 Pocatello 83204 208-232-1114	Southeastern Idaho
Illinois	Association for Child Development P.O. Box 1370 Lagrange Park 60525 708-354-0450	State of Illinois
	Aurora YWCA Child Care Resource, and Referral 201 N. River Aurora 60506 708-897-1363	Kane County
	Child Care Resource and Referral John A. Logan College Carterville 62918 618-985-6384	Fifteen southern counties in Illinois
	Child Care Resource, and Referral of Marion North Rend Lake College, Route 1 Ina 62806 618-437-5321	Clay, Crawford, Edwards, Effingham, Fayette, Jasper, Jefferson, Lawrence, Marion, Richland, Wabash, and Wayne counties

STATE	AGENCY	AREA SERVED
Illinois (*cont.*)	Child Care Resource Service 274 Bevier Hall, 9055 S. Goodwin Urbana 61801 217-333-3252	Champaign, Macon, Vermillion, Piatt, Douglas, and Iroquois counties
	Community Child Care Connection, Inc. 730 East Vine Street #209 Springfield 62703 217-525-2805	Christian, Logan, Macoupin, Menard, Montgomery, Morgan, Sangamon, and Scott counties
	Day Care Action Council 4753 N. Broadway St. #726 Chicago 60640 312-769-8000	Cook County
	Dekalb County Community Coordinated Child Care 145 Fisk Ave. Dekalb 60115 800-848-8727	Dekalb, Ogle, Lee, Whiteside, and Carroll counties
	Illinois Child Care Bureau P.O. Box 2290 Lagrange 60525 708-579-9880	West suburban Cook, Dupage, Will, Lake, Kendall, and McHenry counties
	Jane Addams Child Care 3212 N. Broadway Chicago 60657 312-769-8100	City of Chicago, and suburban Cook County
	The Child Care Connection Illinois Central College East Peoria 61635 309-694-5553	Bureau, Fulton, LaSalle, Marshall, Pazewell, Peoria, Putnam, Stark and Woodford counties

STATE	AGENCY	AREA SERVED
Illinois (*cont.*)	YWCA 220 S. Madison Rockford 61104 815-968-9681	Northwestern Illinois, Boone, Winnebago, Stephenson, and Jo Daviess counties
	YWCA Child Care Resource, and Referral 739 Roosevelt Road Bld 8, #210 Glen Ellyn 60137 708-790-6600	Dupage and Kane counties
	YWCA of Lake County 1900 Grand Avenue Waukegan 60085-3402 708-662-4247	Lake County, expanding to McHenry County
Indiana	Community Coordinated Child Care for The Wabash Valley Inc. 619 Washington Avenue Terre Haute 47802 812-232-3952	Vigo, Clay, Sullivan, Putnam, Vermillion, Greene, Parke, Daviess, Owen, Knox, Fountain, and Montgomery counties
	Community Coordinated Child Care, Inc. 802 No. Lafayette Blvd. South Bend 46601 219-289-7815	St. Joseph County and limited information to other counties in Indiana and Michigan
	Day Care Resources/Human Resources Department P.O. Box 100 Bloomington 47402 812-331-6430	Monroe County
	Day Nursery Association 615 N. Alabama, Suite 108 Indianapolis 46204 317-631-4643	Boone, Hamilton, Hendricks, Marion, Hancock, Morgan, Johnson, and Shelby counties

STATE	AGENCY	AREA SERVED
Indiana (*cont.*)	Tippecanoe County Child Care, Inc. P.O. Box 749 Lafayette 47902 317-742-4033	Tippecanoe, Fountain, Benton, White, Carroll, Clinton, Montgomery, Warren, and Pulaski counties
	YWCA 2000 Wells Street Fort Wayne 46808 219-424-4908	City of Ft. Wayne, and Allen County (northeastern part of state)
	YWCA Child Care Resource and Referral Program 4460 Guion Road Indianapolis 46254 317-299-0626	Marion and surrounding counties
Iowa	Child Care Coordination P.O. Box 4090 Waterloo 50704 319-233-0804	Black Hawk, Tama, Butler, Bremer, Chickasaw, Buchanan, and Grundy counties
	Child Care Resource and Referral 117 North 1st Street Winterset 50273 515-462-1509	Madison and Adair counties
	Child Care Resource and Referral Center P.O. Box 464 Carroll 51401 712-792-6440	Audubon, Carroll, and Sac counties
	Child Care Resource Center 2700 Leech Ave. Sioux City 51106 712-274-2212	Woodbury County

STATE	AGENCY	AREA SERVED
Iowa (*cont.*)	Community Child Care Resource and Referral Center 2804 Eastern Avenue Davenport 52803 319-324-8236	Clinton, Scott, Cedar, and Muscatine counties
	Community Coordinated Child Care 202 S. Linn, P.O. Box 2876 Iowa City 52244 319-338-7684	Johnson County
	Mid-Sioux Opportunity, Inc. 418 Marion Street Remsen 51050 712-786-2001	Plymouth County
	Polk County Child Care Resource Center 1200 University, Suite F Des Moines 50314 515-286-3536	Polk, Warren, Jasper, and Dallas counties
	Project Concern/Phone A Friend, Inc. 2013 Central Avenue Dubuque 52001 319-557-1628	Dubuque County
Kansas	Child Care Association 1069 Parklane Office Park Wichita 67218 316-682-1853	Sedgwick, Harvey, Harper, Sumner, Butler, Kingman, and Cowley counties
	Everywoman's Resource Center 1002 SW Garfield, Suite 109 Topeka 66604 913-357-5171	Topeka and Shawnee counties

STATE	AGENCY	AREA SERVED
Kansas (*cont.*)	Heart of America Family Services 8047 Parallel Parkway Kansas City 66112 816-753-5280	East Central Kansas
Kentucky	Child Care Council of Kentucky 800 Sparta Court, #100 Lexington 40504 606-254-9176	Central Kentucky (twenty-one counties surrounding Fayette County)
	Community Coordinated Child Care 1215 South Third Street Louisville 40203 502-636-1358	Louisville, Jefferson, and surrounding counties
	Kentucky Coalition for School Age Child Care 200 High Street Bowling Green 42101 502-842-4281	State of Kentucky
Louisana	Child Care Information, Inc. P.O. Box 45212, D.223 Baton Rouge 70895 504-293-8523	Twenty-three parishes in central/southern Louisiana
	Child Care Resources P.O. Box 51837 New Orleans 70151 504-586-8509	Greater New Orleans and Lake Charles
	Child Care Services of NW Louisiana 209 Milam, Suite C Shreveport 71101-7728 318-227-1812	North Louisiana

STATE	AGENCY	AREA SERVED
Maine	Bath Brunswick Child Care Services 44 Water Street Brunswick 04011 207-725-6506	Lincoln, Sagadanoc County, and Brunswick area including Harpswell
	Careline Resource Development Center 55 Bowdoin Street P.O. Box 512 Sanford 04083 207-324-0735	York County
	Child Care Connections 87 High Street Portland 04106 207-871-7449	Cumberland County
	Child Care Opportunities P.O. Box 1093 Ellsworth 04605 207-667-2467	Hancock County
	Child Care Resources of Waldo County Route 1, Box 2511 Brooks 04921 800-445-0127	Waldo County
	Downeast Child Care Directory W-HCA Box 280 Milbridge 04658 207-546-7544	Washington County
	Finders/Seekers P.O. Box 278 South Paris 04281 800-543-7008	Oxford, Androscoggin, and Franklin counties

STATE	AGENCY	AREA SERVED
Maine (*cont.*)	Penquis Child Care Resource Development Center 120 Cleveland St. Bangor 04401 207-941-2843	Penebscot, Piscataquis, and Northern Somerset counties
Maryland	Child Care Connection, Inc. 101 Monroe Street Rockville 20850 301-217-1773	Montgomery County
	Child Care Consortium 22 S. Market Street Frederick 21701 301-695-4508	Frederick County
	Maryland Committee for Children 608 Water Street Baltimore 21202 301-625-1111	State of Maryland
	Western Maryland Child Care Resource Center Bryan Centre, 82 W. Washington St., 6th Fl. Hagerstown 21740 301-733-6914	Washington, Garrett, and Alegany counties
Massachusetts	Child Care Circuit 190 Hampshire St. Lawrence 01840 508-686-4288	Tri-city, Eastern Middlesex, North Shore, Cape Ann, and Merrimack valley areas

STATE	AGENCY	AREA SERVED
Massachusetts (*cont.*)	Child Care Connection UWCM—484 Main Street Suite 300 Worcester 01608 508-757-3880	Worcester, Blackstone Valley, and south-central Massachusetts
	Child Care Focus 56 Vernon Street Northampton 01060 413-586-3404	All of Hampshire and Franklin counties, and Athol/Orange area in western Massachusetts
	Child Care Resource Center, Inc. 552 Mass. Avenue Cambridge 02139 617-547-1063	Boston and twelve surrounding towns
	Child Care Resource Exchange Box D-626 4 Park Pl. New Bedford 02742 800-338-1717	Greater New Bedford, Cape, and Islands
	Child Care Resources of Children's Aid, and Family Service, Inc. 344 Main Street Fitchburg 01420 508-343-7395	North Worcester County
	Child Care Search 60 Turner Street Waltham 02154 617-891-4557	Northern and Central Middlesex, and metro area west Boston
	Childcare Resource Connection 17 Tremont Street Taunton 02780 508-823-9118	Greater Fall River area and Greater Taunton area

STATE	AGENCY	AREA SERVED
Massachusetts (*cont.*)	Home/Health and Child Care, Inc. Box 296 Avon 02322 800-222-5609	Greater Brockton, Attleboro, and South Norfolk areas
	PHPCC/Child Care Resource and Referral Consortium 200 Fifth Avenue Waltham 02154 617-890-8781	Arlington, Belmont, Watertown, Lexington, Newton, Wellesley, Brookline, Weston, and Needham
	Preschool Enrichment Team, Inc. 276 High Street Holyoke 01040 413-536-3900	Twenty-one towns with population of half a million
	Quincy Community Action Program 1509 Hancock Street Quincy 02169 617-479-8181	South coastal area of Massachusetts
	Resources for Child Care 311 North Street Pittsfield 01201 413-499-7982	Berkshire County
	Warmlines 492 Waltham Street West Newton 02165 617-244-6843	West suburban area including Newton, Needham, Brookline, Wellsley, Watertown, Waltham, and Weston
Michigan	Child Advocacy Community Coordinated Child Care 150 W. Center Street Alma 48801 517-463-1422	Gratiot, Isabella, and Clare counties

STATE	AGENCY	AREA SERVED
Michigan (*cont.*)	Child Care Coordinating and Referral Service 2454 E. Stadium Blvd. Ann Arbor 48104 313-971-5460	Washtenaw, Lenawee, Monroe, Hillsdale, and Jackson counties
	Child Care Resource and Referral 268-B East Kilgore Kalamazoo 49001 616-346-3296	Kalamazoo, Calhoun, Barry, Branch, Van-buren, and St. Joseph counties
	Community Coordinated Child Care of Detroit/ Wayne County, Inc. 5031 Grandy Detroit 48211 313-579-2777	Wayne County
	Community Coordinated Child Care of the Upper Peninsula 125 W. Washington, Suite F Marquette 49855 906-228-3362	Upper Peninsula of Michigan
	Flint Genesee Community Coordinated Child Care 310 E. Third St., 5th Floor Flint 48502 313-232-0145	Genesee, Lapeer, Tus-cola, Huron, and Sani-lac counties
	Grand Traverse Community Coordinated Child Care Council 1701 East Front Street Traverse City 49684 800-678-4951	Fourteen counties of northwest Michigan

STATE	AGENCY	AREA SERVED
Michigan (*cont.*)	Kent Regional Community Coordinated Child Care 233 E. Fulton, Suite 107 Grand Rapids 49503 616-451-8281	Ionia, Kent, Mecosta, Montcalm, and Osceola counties
	Macomb County Community Coordinated Child Care 21885 Dunham Mt. Clemens 48043 313-469-6993	Macomb and St. Clair counties
	Oakland County Community Coordinated Child Care Council 255 N. Telegraph Road, #206 Waterford 48328 313-858-5140	Oakland and Livingston counties
	Office for Young Children P.O. Box 30161 Lansing 48909 517-887-6996	Ingham, Eaton, Clinton, and Shiawassee counties
	Ottawa County Community Coordinated Child Care 529 East 16th Street Holland 49423 616-396-8151	Ottawa, Allegan, Muskegon, Newaygo, Lake, Mason, and Oceana counties
	Saginaw Valley Regional Community Coordinated Child Care 305 Third Street Freeland 48623 517-695-5080	Arenac, Bay, Midland, and Saginaw counties; Gladwin, Iosco, and Ogemaw

STATE	AGENCY	AREA SERVED
Minnesota	Central Minnesota Child Care Inc. P.O. Box 1797 St. Cloud 56302 612-251-5081	Benton, Stearns, Sherburne, and Wright counties
	Child Care Resource and Referral 1610 Commerce Drive N. Mankato 56001 507-389-5087	Brown, Blue Earth, Faribault, Martin, Nicollet, Sibley, Lesuer, Watonwan, and Waseca counties
	Child Care Resource and Referral, Inc. 2116 Campus Drive SE Rochester 55904 800-462-1660	Rice, Steele, Goodhue, Dodge, Wabasha, Winona, Freeborn, Mower, Fillmore, Houston, and Olmsted counties
	Child Care Resource Center 3602 4th Ave. South Minneapolis 55409 612-823-5261	South Minneapolis
	Community Action Council Child Care Resource and Referral 14451 County Road 11 Burnsville 55337 612-431-7752	Dakota County
	East Central Regional Development Commission 100 South Park Street Mora 55051 800-323-7126	Pine, Mille Lacs, and Kanabec counties

STATE	AGENCY	AREA SERVED
Minnesota (*cont.*)	Greater Minneapolis Day Care Association 1628 Elliot Ave. South Minneapolis 55404 612-341-2066	Hennepin County
	Heartland Community Action Agency, Inc. P.O. Box 1359 Willmar 56201 612-235-0850	Kandiyohi, Mcleod, Meeker, and Renville counties
	Lakes and Prairies Child Care Resource and Referral P.O. Box 919 Moorhead 56560 507-233-7514	Nine counties: Becker, Clay, Douglas, Grant, Pope, Ottertail, Stevens, Travers, Wilkin, and Cass counties in North Dakota
	Minnesota Child Care Innovations, Inc. 12700 Nicollet Ave. So. #204 Burnsville 55337 612-894-0727	State of Minnesota
	Parenting Resource Center, Inc. Box 505 Austin 55912 507-433-0692	Mower and Freeborn counties
	Prairie Five Community Action Council P.O. Box 695 Montevideo 56265 507-269-6578	Big Stone, Chippewa, Lacqui, Parle, Swift, and Yellow Medicine counties
	Resources for Child Caring 450 N. Syndicate, Suite 5 St. Paul 55119 612-641-0332	Ramsey County

STATE	AGENCY	AREA SERVED
Minnesota (*cont.*)	Scope Resource Center 122 E. McKinley Owatonna 55060 507-455-2560	Steele County
	The Family Resource Center P.O. Box 836 Lindstrom 55045 612-257-2400	Chisago and Isanti counties
	Tri Valley Child Care Resource and Referral, Inc. Box 607 Crookston 56716 218-281-6672	Kittson, Roseau, Marshall, Polk, Pennington, Red Lake, and Norman counties in Minnesota; Grand Forks in North Dakota
	Washington County Child Care Resource and Referral 14900 61st St. N Stillwater 55082 612-779-5023	Washington County
Missouri	Child Day Care Association 915 Olive—Suite 913 St. Louis 63101 314-241-3161	Missouri: St. Louis, St. Charles, Jefferson, and Franklin counties. Illinois: St. Clair, Madison, Monroe, Randolph, Washington, Bond, Clinton, Perry, and Fayette counties
	Heart of America Family Services 3217 Broadway #500 Kansas City 64111 816-753-5280	Greater Kansas City area

STATE	AGENCY	AREA SERVED
Montana	Child Care Connections 321 E. Main #423 Bozeman 59715 406-587-7786	Gallatin, Park, and Meagher counties
	Human Resources Development Council P.O. Box 2016 Billings 59103 406-248-1477	Big Horn, Carbon, Stillwater, Sweetgrass, and Yellowstone counties
Nebraska	Midwest Child Care Association 5015 Dodge #2 Omaha 68132 402-551-2379	State of Nebraska and a small part of Iowa
Nevada	Child Care Resource Council 1090 South Rock Boulevard Reno 89502 702-785-4200	Washoe County, Carson City, incline Village, and other close outlying rural areas
New Hampshire	Child and Family Services of New Hampshire 99 Hanover Street Manchester 03105 603-668-1920	Greater Manchester area, N. Hillsboro County, and Concord areas
	Rockingham County Child Care Services 287 Lawrence Road Salem 03079 603-893-8413	Rockingham County
	University of New Hampshire, O'Kane House Child Care Resource and Referral Durham 03824 603-862-2895	Strafford County, Seacoast, and Rockingham County

STATE	AGENCY	AREA SERVED
New Jersey	Atlantic County Women's Center P.O. Box 311 Northfield 08225 609-646-1180	Atlantic County
	Bergen County Office for Children 21 Main Street Hackensack 07601 201-646-3694	Bergen County
	Camden County Division for Children 1300 Admiral Wilson Boulevard Camden 08101 609-968-4260	Camden County
	Child Care Channels 700 Sayre Avenue Phillipsburg 08865 201-454-2074	Warren County
	Children's Home Society Child Care 929 Parkside Avenue Trenton 08618 908-505-1133	Ocean County
	Children's Services of Morris County 855 Rt. 10 East, #114 Randolph 07869 201-927-6060	Morris County
	Community Coordinated Child Care 60 Prince Street Elizabeth 07208 201-353-1621	Union County, Middle-sex, and Ocean County

STATE	AGENCY	AREA SERVED
New Jersey (*cont.*)	Passaic County Child Care Coordinating Agency, Inc. 262 Main St., 5th Floor Paterson 07505 201-684-1904	Hudson, Passaic, and Sussex counties
	Programs for Parents, Inc. 56 Grove Avenue Verona 07042 201-857-5171	Suburban Essex County
	Southern Regional Child Care Resource Center (EIRC) 700 Hollydell Court Sewell 08080 609-582-8282	Cape May, Gloucester, and Salem counties
	The Child Care Connection, Inc. 2425 Pennington Road Trenton 08638 609-737-2418	Mercer and Somerset counties
	The Work-Family Consortium, Inc. P.O. Box 881 Flemington 08822 908-788-8600	Hunterdon County
	United Way of Monmouth County 1415 Wycoff Road Farmingdale 07727 908-938-2250	Monmouth County
New Mexico	Child Care Resource and Referral Project/Santa Fe Community College P.O. Box 4187 Santa Fe 87502-4187 505-438-1344	Santa Fe, Los Alamos, and Espanola counties

STATE	AGENCY	AREA SERVED
New Mexico (*cont.*)	Las Cruces Child Care Resource and Referral Box 30001, Dept 3R Las Cruces 88003 505-646-1165	Greater Las Cruces Area
	Roswell Child Care Resource and Referral, Inc. P.O. Box 3038 Roswell 88202 505-622-9000	Primarily Chaves County, but referrals can be made throughout southeast New Mexico
New York	Broome County Child Development Council, Inc. 29 Fayette St. P.O. 880 Binghamton 13902-0880 607-723-8313	Broome and Tioga counties
	Capital District Child Care Coordinating Council, Inc. 352 Central Ave. Albany 12206 518-426-7181	Albany, Schenectady, Rensselaer, and Saratoga counties
	Child Care Coalition of Niagara Frontier, Inc. 656 Elmwood Ave. Buffalo 14222 716-882-6544	Erie and Niagara counties
	Child Care Council of Suffolk, Inc. 145 Pidgeon Hill Road Huntington Station 11746 516-427-1206	Suffolk County
	Child Care Council of Westchester, Inc. 470 Mamaroneck Avenue White Plains 10605 914-761-3456	Westchester County

STATE	AGENCY	AREA SERVED
New York (*cont.*)	Child Care, Inc. 275 Seventh Ave. New York 10001 212-929-4999	New York City—all five boroughs
	Child Development Support Corporation P.O. Box 474258 Brooklyn 11247 718-398-2050	Five boroughs of New York City
	Cortland Area Child Care Council, Inc. 111 Port Watson Street Cortland 13059 607-753-0106	Cortland County
	Day Care and Child Development Council of Tompkins County, Inc. 609 W. Clinton Street Ithaca 14850 607-273-0259	Tompkins County
	Day Care Council of Nassau County, Inc. 54 Washington St. Hempstead 11550 516-538-1362	Nassau County
	Delaware Opportunities, Inc. 47 Main Street Delhi 13753 607-746-2165	Delaware County
	Dutchess County Child Development Council, Inc. 53 Academy Street Poughkeepsie 12601 914-473-4141	Dutchess County

STATE	AGENCY	AREA SERVED
New York (*cont.*)	EOP Child Care Resource Development Program Elmira College Box 855 Elmira 14901 607-734 3941	Chemung County
	Onondaga County Child Care Council 215 Bassett Street Syracuse 13210 315-472-6919	Onondaga County

	Parent Resource Center
	165 Charles Street
	Painted Post
	14870
	607-936-3704
		Steuben County, with
		  particular attention to
		  Corning School Dis-
		  trict

	Putnam County Child Care Council 73 Gleneida Avenue Carmel 10512 914-228-1994	Putnam County
	Rockland Council for Young Children 185 North Main Street Spring Valley 10977 914-425-0572	Rockland County
	Steuben Day Care Project/SCEOP P.O. Box 352 Bath 14810 607-776-2125	Steuben County
	Sullivan County Child Care Council P.O. Box 864 Liberty 12754 914-292-7166	Sullivan County

STATE	AGENCY	AREA SERVED
New York (*cont.*)	Western New York Child Care Council, Inc. 1344 University Avenue Rochester 14607 800-333-0825	Monroe, Wayne, Ontario, Yates, Wyoming, Allegheny, Livingston, Orleans, Genesee counties
North Carolina	Child Care Connections of Moore County, Inc. P.O. Box 938 Carthage 28327 919-947-2687	Moore County
	Child Care Directions P.O. Box 911 Laurinburg 28353 919-276-3367	Scotland, Robeson, Cumberland, Hoke and Richmond counties
	Child Care Information Program 1200 Arlington Street Greensboro 27406 919-378-7700	Guilford, Forsyth, Rockingham, Randolph, Stokes, Yadkin, David, and Davidson counties (triad area)
	Child Care Networks 222 Carr Mill Carrboro 27510 919-942-0184	Orange and Chatham counties
	Child Care Resource and Referral of Wake County 103 Enterprise St., #209 Raleigh 27607 919-821-0482	Wake, Franklin, Harnett, and Johnston counties
	Child Care Resources, Inc. 700 Kenilworth Avenue Charlotte 28204 704-376-6697	Mecklenburg, Union, and Cabarrus counties

STATE	AGENCY	AREA SERVED
North Carolina (*cont.*)	Durham Day Care Council 119 Orange Street Durham 27701 919-688-9550	Durham and Granville counties
	SE Community College Child Care Resource and Referral P.O. Box 151 Whiteville 28472 919-642-7141	Southeastern North Carolina (Columbus, Bladen, and Pender counties)
North Dakota	Early Childhood Training Center, NDSU P.O. Box 5057, State Univ. Station Fargo 58105 701-237-8040	State of North Dakota
Ohio	Action for Children 92 Jefferson Avenue Columbus 43215 614-224-0222	Franklin County
	Center for Alternative Resources P.O. Box 77 Newark 43055 614-345-6166	Licking County
	Child Care Clearinghouse 414 Valley Street Dayton 45404 513-461-0600	Montgomery, Greene, Preble, Miami, Clark, and Warren counties
	Child Care Insights, Inc. 19111 Detroit Rd #104 Rocky River 44116 216-356-2900	All of Ohio and parts of Pennsylvania

STATE	AGENCY	AREA SERVED
Ohio (*cont.*)	Child Care Resource Ceenter 385 Midway Blvd, #312 Elyria 44035 216-324-7187	Lorain County
	Child Care Resource Center 3135 Euclid, Suite 302 Cleveland 44115 216-431-1818	Greater Cleveland area and surrounding sub-urbs
	Community Coordinated Child Care 1225 East McMillan Cincinnati 45206 513-221-0033	Boone, Kenton, Camp-bell, counties in Ken-tucky; Hamilton, Clermont, Butler, and Warren counties in Ohio; Dearborn County in Indiana
	Info Line 474 Grant Street Akron 44311 216-376-7706	Summit County
	Northwestern Ohio Community Action Commission 1933 E. Second Street Defiance 43512 419-784-2150	Williams, Fulton, Henry, Defiance, Paulding counties
	YW Child Care Connections 1018 Jefferson Ave. Toledo 43624 419-255-5519	Toledo area, northwest Ohio, lower southeast Michigan
Oklahoma	Child Care Connection 3014 Paseo Oklahoma City 73103 405-525-3111	Metro Oklahoma City, Canadian, Lincoln, Oklahoma, Cleveland, Pottawatomi, and Logan counties

STATE	AGENCY	AREA SERVED
Oklahoma (*cont.*)	Child Care Resource Center 1430 South Boulder Tulsa 74119 918-587-care	Eleven counties around Tulsa
Oregon	Linn and Benton Child Care Resource and Referral 6500 SW Pacific Boulevard Albany 97321 503-967-6501	Linn and Beton counties
	Metro Child Care Resource and Referral P.O. Box 16521 Portland 97216 503-256-5484	Multnomah, Clackamas, and Washington coun- ties, including the metro Portland area
	Mid Willamette Child Care Information Service 325 13th St. NE #206 Salem 97301 503-585-2491	Marion, Polk, and Yam- hill counties
	UCAN's Child Care Resource and Referral 2448 W. Harvard Blvd. Roseburg 97470 503-672-7004	Douglas County
	West Tuality Child Care Services, Inc. 2813 Pacific Ave. #C Forest Grove 97116 503-357-4994	Washington County
Pennsylvania	Child Care Choices 125 S 9th St., #603 Philadelphia 19107 215-592-7644	Philadelphia, Montgom- ery, Bucks, Chester, and Delaware counties

STATE	AGENCY	AREA SERVED
Pennsylvania (*cont.*)	Child Care Consultants, Inc. 376 East Market Street York 17403 717-854-care	Adams, Franklin, Lancaster, York counties, and south central Pennsylvania
	Child Placement Network, Inc. 2720 Potshop Road Norristown 19403 215-584-0960	Lehigh County, Bucks, Berks, Montgomery, Chester, and Delaware counties
	Community Services for Children, Inc. 431 East Locust Street Bethlehem 18018 215-tot-info	Northampton, Carbon, and Monroe counties. Secondary areas include northeastern Pennsylvania counties
	Delaware Valley Child Care Resource and Referral Center 840 W. Main St, 3rd Floor Lansdale 19446 800-vip-kids	Delaware: New Castle County. Pennsylvania: Bucks, Montgomery, Chester, Delaware, Berks, Philadelphia. New Jersey: Burlington, Gloucester, and Camden counties
	International Institute of Erie P.O. Box 486 Erie 16512 814-452-3935	Erie County
	Probe 3400 Trindle Road Camp Hill 17011 717-737-2584	Dauphin, Cumberland, Perry, York, Adams, Lancaster, and Lebanon counties
	United Way's Child Care Network 200 Ross St., #600, 5th Fl. Pittsburgh 15219 412-392-3131	Allegheny, Beaver, Butler, Westmoreland, and Washington counties (plus nine southwestern counties)

STATE	AGENCY	AREA SERVED
Rhode Island	Options for Working Parents 30 Exchange Terrace Providence 02903 401-272-7510	State of Rhode Island
South Carolina	Child Care Options, Inc. 1521 Wappoo Raod Charleston 29407 803-556-5706	Charleston, Berkeley, Bufort, Horry, Dorchester, and Colleton
	Childcare and Seniorcare Solutions P.O. Box 24617 Columbia 29224 803-736-7652	Greater Columbia, Lexington, and Blythewood
	Greenville's Child, Inc. P O. Box 8821 Greenville 29604 803-242-8320	Greenville, Spartanburg, Abbeville, Anderson, Cherokee, Chester, Greenwood, Lancaster, Laurens, Ocoree, Pickens, Union counties
	Yes, Inc. 2129 Santee Avenue Columbia 29205 803-254-9263	Twenty-six counties in the Midlands of South Carolina
South Dakota	Child Development and Family Relations Box 2218, SDSU Brookings 57007 605-688-5730	Brookings County
	Positive Parent Network P.O. Box 2792 Rapid City 57709 605-348-9276	Rapid City area

STATE	AGENCY	AREA SERVED
Tennessee	Tennessee Child Care Resoruce and Referral Services TN DHS/Day Care Services Nashville 37248-9600 615-741-0290	State of Tennessee
Texas	Austin Families, Inc. 3305 Northland Dr., #410 Austin 78731 512-454-1195	Austin, metro area and central Texas
	Child Care Answers 1499 Regal Row #400 Dallas 75247 214-631-care	Dallas/Ft.Worth Metro-plex, 31-county area in North Central Texas
	Children's Enterprises, Inc. 3305 66th Street, Suite 1 Lubbock 79413 806-796-0734	106 counties in West Texas
	Initiatives for Children, Inc. 5433 Westheimer, #620 Houston 77056 713-840-1255	Thirteen counties in greater Houston area
	Kid Care 115 Plaza De Armas, #240 San Antonio 78205 512-227-help	Bexar County
	MTX Day Care Services, Inc. 523 West 1st Ave. Corsicana 75110 214-872-5231	Ellis, Kaufman, and Navarro counties

STATE	AGENCY	AREA SERVED
Texas (*cont.*)	YWCA of El Paso 1918 Texas El Paso 79901 915-533-7475	El Paso County
Utah	Children First 5215 Greenpine Drive Murray 84123 801-268-9492	Salt Lake and Utah County
	Children's Service Society 576 East South Temple Salt Lake City 84102 801-537-1044	Wasalch Front, Ogden to Provo with most referrals in Salt Lake City
Vermont	Child Care Information Service Vermont College Montpelier 05602 802-828-8771	Washington and Lomoille counties
	Child Care Resource and Referral of Chittenden County 179 S. Winooski Ave. Burlington 05401 802-863-3367	Chittenden County
Virginia	CVCDA/office for Children and Youth 810 E. High Street Charlottesville 22902 804-977-4260	Charlottesville; Albermarie, Greene, Louisa, Fluvanna, Nelson counties
	Fairfax County Office for Children 3701 Pender Drive Fairfax 22030 703-359-5860	Fairfax County

STATE	AGENCY	AREA SERVED
Virginia (*cont.*)	Kare Line Child Care Resource and Referral 1010 Miller Park Square Lynchburg 24501 804-846-4630	Amherst, Appomattox, Bedford, and Campbell counties; cities of Lynchburg and Bedford; town of Altavista
	Memorial Child Guidance Clinic 5001 W. Broad Street #217 Richmond 23230 804-282-5993	Richmond City, Petersburg, counties of Hanover, Goochland, Henrico, Chesterfield, New Kent, Charles City, and Chester
	Next Door Child Care Program 7511 Fordson Road Alexandria 22306 703-765-0925	Route One Corridor of Alexandria
	The Child Caring Connection 109 Cary Street, #201 Williamsburg 23185 804-229-7940	Williamsburgh, James City County, Bruton District of York
	The Planning Council 130 West Plume Street Norfolk 23510 804-627-3993	Norfolk, Virginia Beach, Portsmouth, Chesapeake, Suffolk, Franklin, Ile of Wright, peninsula cities, and counties, E. Shore, and Prince William County
	Virginia Tech Resource and Referral Service 201 Church St. Blacksburg 24061-0537 703-231-3213	Blacksburg, Christiansburg, Radford, New River Valley Area

STATE	AGENCY	AREA SERVED
Washington	Child and Family Resource and Referral 15015 Main Street, #206 Bellevue 98007 206-865-9350	Metropolitan Seattle area and King County
	Child Care Action Council P.O. Box 446 Olympia 98507-0446 206-754-0810	Thurston County
	Child Care Resource and Referral 1313 NE 134th Street Vancouver 98685 206-574-6826	Clark County
	Child Care Support Services Resource and Referral 720 West Court Pasco 99301 509-547-1718	Benton-Franklin counties (lower) Yakima County, and (western) Walla Walla County
	Daycare Placement Services P.O. Box 435 Issaquah 98027 206-391-9549	Issaquah, Redmond, Fall City, Kirkland, Bethell, Bellevue, Renton, and North Bend
	Volunteers of America/Child Care Resource and Referral Network 2802 Broadway Everett 98201 206-258-4213	Snohomish County
	Washington State University Child Care Resource and Referral 103 Commons Hall, WSU Pullman 99164-3610 509-335-7625	City of Pullman

STATE	AGENCY	AREA SERVED
West Virginia	Central Child Care of West Virginia, Inc. 1205 Quarrier Street Charleston 25361 304-340-3667	State of West Virginia
Wisconsin	Child Care Information and Referral Service, Inc. P.O. Box 4521 Appleton 54915 414-734-0966	Outagamie County

	Child Care Partnership Resource and Referral
	P.O. Box 45
	Independence
	54747
	715-985-2391
		Buffalo, Eau Claire,
		   Jackson, and Trem-
		   pealeau counties

	Child Care Resource and Referral Center of Wood County 122 8th St. S Wisconsin Rapids 54494 715-423-4114	Wood County
	Child Care Resource and Referral of Racine 5420 21st Street Racine 53406 414-554-4698	Racine County
	Community Action Resource and Referral— Walworth Co. 910 East Geneva St., P.O. Box 362 Delavan 53115 414-728-8780	Walworth County

STATE	AGENCY	AREA SERVED
Wisconsin (*cont.*)	Community Coordinated Child Care of Milwaukee County, Inc. 2001 W. Vliet Street Milwaukee 53205 414-933-kids	Milwaukee, Waukesha, Ozaukee, and Washington counties
	Dane County Community Coordinated Child Care 3200 Monroe Street Madison 53711 608-238-7338	Dane County
	Family Connections Resource and Referral 310 Bluff Ave. Sheboygan 53081 414-457-1999	Sheboygan County
	Partners in Care Resource and Referral P.O. Box 242 Depere 54115 414-432-7706	Brown County
	Resource and Referral Center 8600 Sheridan Road Kenosha 53140 414-697-2529	Kenosha County
Wyoming	Day Care Resource and Referral Service 625 South Beverly Casper 82609 307-472-5535	Natrona County

Appendix 4

Child Care Resource and Referral Agencies—Statewide Networks

STATE	AGENCY	AREA SERVED
Alabama	Alabama Association for Child Care Resource and Referral Agencies 309 North 23rd Street Birmingham 35203 205-252-1991	State of Alabama
Alaska	Alaska Child Care Resource and Referral Alliance P.O. Box 10339 Anchorage 99510 907-279-5024	State of Alaska
California	California Child Care Resource and Referral Network 809 Lincoln Way San Francisco 94122 415-661-1714	State of California
Colorado	Colorado Child Care Resource and Referral Network 5675 S. Academy Boulevard Colorado Springs 80906 719-540-7252	State of Colorado

STATE	AGENCY	AREA SERVED
Florida	Florida Child Care Resource and Referral Network 1282 Paul Russell Road Tallahassee 32301 904-656-2272	State of Florida
Illinois	Illinois Child Care Resource and Referral System 100 W. Randolph, Suite 16-206 Chicago 60601 312-814-5524	State of Illinois
Indiana	Indiana Association for Child Care Resource and Referral 4460 Guion Road Indianapolis 46254 317-299-2750	State of Indiana
Iowa	Iowa Commission On Children, Youth and Families Dept. of Human Rights/Lucas Building Des Moines 50319 515-281-3974	State of Iowa
Maine	Maine Association of Child Care Resource and Referral Agencies P.O. Box 280—WHCA Milbridge 04658 207-546-7544	State of Maine
Maryland	Maryland Child Care Resource Network 608 Water Street Baltimore 21202 301-752-7588	State of Maryland

STATE	AGENCY	AREA SERVED
Massachusetts	Massachusetts Office for Children 10 West Street, 5th Floor Boston 02111 617-727-8900	State of Massachusetts
Michigan	Michigan Community Coordinated Child Care (4C) Association 2875 Northwind Dr. #200 East Lansing 48823 517-351-4171	State of Michigan
Minnesota	Minnesota Child Care Resource and Referral Network 2116 Campus Drive SE Rochester 55904 507-287-2497	State of Minnesota
New Hampshire	New Hampshire Assoc. of Child Care Resource and Referral Agencies 99 Hanover Street, P.O. Box 448 Manchester 03105 603-668-1920	State of New Hampshire
New Jersey	Statewide Clearinghouse/Div. of Youth and Family Services Capitol Center, 50 E. State Street, CN 717 Trenton 08625 609-292-8408	State of New Jersey
New York	New York State Child Care Coordinating Council 237 Bradford Street Albany 12206 518-463-8663	State of New York

STATE	AGENCY	AREA SERVED
North Carolina	North Carolina Child Care Resource and Referral Network 700 Kenilworth Avenue Charlotte 28204 704-376-6697	State of North Carolina
Ohio	Ohio Child Care Resource and Referral Association 92 Jefferson Avenue Columbus 43215 614-224-0222	State of Ohio
Oregon	Oregon Child Care Resource and Referral Network 325 13th St. NE, #206 Salem 97301 503-585-6232	State of Oregon
South Carolina	South Carolina Child Care Resource and Referral Network 2129 Santee Avenue Columbia 29205 803-254-9263	State of South Carolina
Texas	Texas Association of Child Care Resource and Referral Agencies 4029 Capital of Texas Highway S., Suite 102 Austin 78704 512-440-8555	State of Texas
Vermont	Vermont Association of Child Care Resource and Referral Agencies Early Childhood Programs/Vermont College Montpelier 05602 802-828-8675	State of Vermont

STATE	AGENCY	AREA SERVED
Virginia	Virginia Child Care Resource and Referral Network 3701 Pender Drive Fairfax 22030 703-218-3730	State of Virginia
Washington	Washington State Child Care Resource and Referral Network P.O. Box 1241 Tacoma 98401 206-383-1735	State of Washington
Wisconsin	Wisconsin Child Care Improvement Project 315 W 5, P.O. Box 369 Hayward 54843 715-634-3905	State of Wisconsin

Index